SEX T

KIM SCAPA was educated at a minor public school in England, then at prep school in Pennsylvania. He is now a professional tennis coach and resides in Encino, California.

He is partly responsible for 'punk tennis' (slashed tracksuits, bondage shorts) which swept the local park courts around the West Coast in 1979. His greatest achievement was to have a tan all year in 1981; his greatest failure, Francesca Holland at Nicholas Straker's party, Forest Hill, 1978.

SEX TIPS FOR BOYS

Kim Scapa

Published by Arrow Books in 1993
7 9 11 13 15 14 12 10 8

First published in the United Kingdom in 1986 by
Arrow Books
Random House, 20 Vauxhall Bridge Road, London SW1V 2SA

Random House Australia (Pty) Limited
20 Alfred Street, Milsons Point, Sydney,
New South Wales 2061, Australia

Random House New Zealand Limited
18 Poland Road, Glenfield
Auckland 10, New Zealand

Random House South Africa (Pty) Limited
PO Box 337, Bergvlei, South Africa

Random House UK Limited Reg. No. 954009

A CIP catalogue record for this book
is available from the British Library

ISBN 0 09 945160 3

Printed and bound by Firmin-Didot (France),
Group Herissey. No d'impression : 29726.

Prologue

Vale do Lobo, Portugal

It had been another long, hot day on the courts. The day started at eight o'clock, as it did in most Southern European tennis resorts, progressed with solid lessons until twelve noon, then broke for four hours before going on again until seven p.m. It had been a good day – the weather was clear and hot, the punters were burnt and happy, and the team of pros were tanned and impressive. But the head pro, a thirty-year-old veteran, one of Banstead's finest, was worried. 'Things are changing,' he explained, his moustache and attractively sun-blistered lip curling over the frosted rim of a lime juice and Perrier. 'Young guys just aren't the same any more.' He gestured at his team of pros, vacationing university players, now oiling themselves down for the benefit of the unashamedly staring female punters. 'Oh, sure, they look the part, but they've lost that instinctive sense of purpose. We hire them for three things, to look athletic, to teach tennis, and to sleep with the female guests. That's not shocking, it's a fact of resort life. The young guys today look better than ever, play fantastically, but they're not so good with the girls any more. They've lost their confidence. It's worrying.'

Palm Beach, Florida

She sat back on her sun mat and shut her eyes again. Her hair was bleached golden blonde in a natural parody of heavy salon highlights, her skin was a rich caramel brown, her slender bathing costume so abundantly filled that even the lifeguards blushed when they spoke to her. 'I'm not embarrassed about it,' she took her Diet Coke out of the cooler and rolled it languidly across her stomach leaving two lines of beaded moisture. 'They call me the sure thing, after that movie. And I am. I like making it with boys. But it isn't like it was. Young guys have the looks, and the energy, some of them are pretty experienced, but they've just lost their cool. I mean seriously. They need help.'

Smith's Lawn, Windsor Great Park

She was a Sloane heart throb, straight blonde hair, liquid blue eyes, gently tanned skin, boyish athletic figure. At her twenty-first Jennifer had described her as 'the prettiest young thing in London'. 'I'm not going to make a big thing about this,' she pushed her Vuarnet sunglasses up in one smooth, well-practised manoeuvre, instantly converting them into a Polaroid hairband. 'But I've had four boyfriends in the last twelve months, all under thirty, all intolerable. They're just so worried about things. They ruin everything. Now I stick to the very rich, much older, Latins. They can be bores but at least they're more manly.'

What's going on?

Women have always been perplexing creatures. Since the dawning of pre-history man has found them excruciatingly difficult to understand, let alone ask out, kiss, and try and take to bed. But over the last ten years things have got really bad. Knowing when to try a first kiss, when to touch their breasts, how to ask them to do oral sex, or whether they're using a contraceptive have always been issues fraught with complexity, riddled with embarrassment. But modern man seems to be losing his ability to cope, to shrug it off. He's wimping out.

Why?

Let's begin with a little history.

You and Your Erection – a brief history

Two thousand years ago erections roamed the earth unperturbed, unconfused, clear-sighted, upstanding, proud and praised. There was no Desmond Morris man-watching them, there was no Shere Hite codefying the female response to them and their owners' application of them. They just got on with things, they rose and fell with the tide and the moon, and everyone felt good. Tumescence was considered a good thing, a manly thing. Men smiled when it happened. Women clapped. They painted cave walls and hunted dinosaur in simple, unassuming contentment. When Raquel Welch and her breasts starred in *2000 Years BC* youthful cavemen didn't shudder and, like their management consultancy counterparts from modern day Maida Vale, start worrying about what to do if they got an erection in their skin-tight loincloths. They just sat back and enjoyed things, calm in the knowledge they didn't have to pretend it was just the ribbing in the cloth.

Then somebody invented a god. His friends chipped in with a few more gods, and pretty soon a whole panoply of gods was looking down, watching, manoeuvring, laughing and cheating. The heavens strained under their weight, man couldn't move for their nosiness. Hunting dinosaur, painting caves, even getting off with women was suddenly less leisurely and more complex. Sacrifices had to be made, gods had to be asked and appeased, heterosexual life in the caves became tougher. But things were basically still cool. Because the gods were still one of the boys, part of the gang, kids on the block. They wanted the same sort of things. They wanted to get off with the same women, they were unfaithful to their wives, they got girls pregnant, they even had erections. The competition had hotted up, but the game stayed basically the same.

Time passed. The Stone Age became the Iron Age, Abyssinians, Turks, Greeks and Romans advanced and retreated then, from nowhere, came God with a capital 'G', a singular, all-powerful God, and the game completely changed. This God didn't act like the other ones. He didn't chase girls, he didn't loiter round late at night. After a bit he didn't even get pissed off. He just sat upstairs and watched, a celestial voyeur. And erections everywhere wilted under the pressure. God-fearing men who once hadn't thought twice about the occasional stiffness in their trousers were now having to get down on their knees and apologize for it. Original fun became original sin. Conscience was born, the most powerful anti-aphrodisiac yet known to man. Once-cheerful erections were driven, flushed with embarrassment, into the bathroom. Having sex was bad full stop. Having it with your wife just about okay providing it was grit your teeth and bear it style and strictly for producing kids. Before marriage, outside of marriage, or for fun in marriage, you were talking in terms of hell-fire and brimstone.

The advance of sexual guilt was spectacular. With the bedroom sewn up, it turned to the bathroom, the first refuge of the hunted erection. The unassuming hand-shandy was branded 'SELF-ABUSE', and by the end of the Middle Ages it too was a heavy sin, actually incurring more brimstone points than sleeping with your sister or being adulterous with your wife.

For 1500 years the shocked erection stayed locked in the closet. It refused to go away, it still provided generations of owners hours of pleasure and satisfaction, but it always came mixed with lashings of embarrassment and pangs of guilt.

Then came Rock 'n' Roll, swiftly followed by the swinging sixties, and flower power. Elvis discovered the groin again, and singers everywhere followed his example singing and dancing from this long-neglected zone. Trousers got tighter, hair got longer, love became cooler, and finally free, the bikini was invented, the Pill, and the orgy was re-established. In the world's musky closets erections began to stir, and gingerly peep out from behind their shrouds of guilt and pubic hair.

All of a sudden they were beginning to have a good time again.

But it was painfully shortlived. No sooner had they got used to roaming the old pastures than Feminism happened, and Women's Lib put them back in their chains. All the old feelings of guilt rushed back, except this time wanting a girl to dress up in stockings and suspenders wasn't just a 'dirty thought', it was a reactionary political gesture of male dominance. Political was added to religious guilt.

Erections were slammed back in their closets while their owners tried to teach them to be enlightened, to forget about French Maid's uniforms and having sex in lifts. Instinct was forced into the straitjacket of the New Man. He liked quiche, he was happy to stay at home while his wife worked. In spirit he was a breastfeeder, even though he couldn't actually do it in practice.

That was tough. Things were to get worse.

Women started breaking into men's jobs, driving men's cars, taking men's holidays, playing men's sports. Worse, they turned out to be better at them. Suddenly average man was faced with trying to make passes at women who not only demanded enlightenment, but also drove bigger cars, had nicer flats, were paid more for doing more exciting jobs. He felt small, left out, unsure. Women were now terrifying combinations of all that was most frightening about women, and all that was most frightening about men.

Erections withered. Women became sexual guerillas.

They had TV programmes for each other, they wrote books for each other, they had discussion classes (*Flirting – the dos and don'ts with the modern man. How to make a man fall in love, Sex Tips for Girls, Married Men*). In each case men were considered hopelessly confused, permanently lost, shrinking reactionary souls.

But their erections were still important.

How was the erection to be saved before the crumbling male psyche lost it altogether?

STOP!

This train of thought is a terribly dangerous one. The onus of responsibility is being given to the wrong people. No matter how fond they are of them, erections can't be left to women. Erections are men's business, men's responsibility. They must learn to get their nerve back, to understand what the women are trying to do, and to do it to them first.

A Basic Rule

Women and men look at sex very differently.

Take a look at a letter, written by an ordinary man to an ordinary men's magazine (nude girls, convertible cars, motorbike reports), describing his sexual fantasy.

Dear Ed

I think your magazine is great. My wife and I enjoy it together whenever we can. But please can we have more pictures of girls with big tits in peep-hole bras. That would give me a real stiffy. Anyway, that reminds me of the time when I got drunk with a few of my mates from the office and came home to find my wife Brenda (name changed) wearing her really tiny négligée watching a dirty video.

My mates got really excited and so did my wife who didn't expect us home so early. 'I don't usually do this,' she said. I then just happened to mention that my friend John (name changed) used to be called Big Dong at school when we saw him in the showers. My wife said, 'Really,' and I said, 'Yeah,' and then, 'Go on John.'

It didn't take John a second to unzip his huge, already hardening cock. 'Mmmh,' said Brenda. I winked at her and in a moment she was kneeling in front of John taking his elephantine knob into her wide-open mouth. Terry and Dave (names changed) by this time were naked. Terry got down behind Brenda, pulled off her skimpy knickers and slid his throbbing love-stick into her squelching fanny. 'Mmmh,' moaned Brenda. As soon as John shot his load Dave took his place and buried his truncheon in my wife's face. Then they all fell in a heap on the rug.

When my mates had gone Brenda and me went to bed and had amazing sex after we talked about what had happened. It was fantastic.

Contrast that with a section from a major romantic novel, the female fantasy.

The waves crashed onto the sand a little way out from where Charlotte was standing, then slid up the shingle hissing loudly. The palms shook in the night breeze. The moonlight bathed everything in eery luminous white. She could feel her heart throbbing in expectation. Suddenly she felt him. Felt his presence. She spun round and looked up. He was standing on the cliff top, his strong, gaunt silhouette looking intensely out to sea, out to that forgotten past which he would never share but whose pain would never leave. Before she knew what she was doing Charlotte had started to run, wildly, desperately towards him.

The wind seemed to whip about her face louder and faster, the waves to crash more thunderously on the sand. He continued to stare out into the darkness until suddenly he heard her coming, looked down, and he too started to run. Charlotte fell into his arms and his lips began to graze the soft skin around the nape of her neck, then her cheeks, and finally the full softness of her mouth. She reached for him as he crushed her in the passion of his embrace and as their kisses grew in intensity Charlotte felt a bead of moisture on her silk ball gown. Then another. She pulled away for a moment and looked at him, his broad shoulders, windswept hair and wide, kind face and realized that he was crying. She sighed with the emotion and grabbed him again, holding his head to her breasts, vowing that they would never be apart again.

Two million men buy *Men Only* every month. A similar number of women buy a pound and a half of the latest romantic fiction. To say that a gulf separates men from women when it comes to sex is like saying Scunthorpe isn't really the same as Honolulu. That gulf is an abyss, a black hole, a whole universe. Light years separate the sexes. Somehow we've got to bridge that gap. To project the right image across that void.

Where do we begin?

Sex tip no. 1: Where Did Sex Come From?

Romantics writing about great lovers always have the starry-eyed pair petting away, convinced that no other human beings have ever felt or touched this way in the history of the Penge Odeon back row. Cliché that it is, romantically speaking, it does raise an interesting question, which is, if we didn't invent all these curious sexual practices, who did?

Now some of the current lexicon of sexual variety has just got to be modern. Victorian lovers couldn't have dressed up in PVC outfits or rubber stockings, but that's really more accessory sex which is small-fry compared to the major moves. I mean who discovered the clitoris? Who gave the first blow-job? Who invented the missionary position? How did it all come about?

They all seem such unlikely activities that you can't help feeling they must have been fairly recent inventions – a product of modern decadence rather than ancient innocence. Yet astonishingly the Ancients, for all their technological backwardness, needed no help when it came to sex. They had no dirty mags, no dirty videos, no bike sheds to gossip behind. Yet they came up with the goods.

Biblical scholars and romantic poets say it was the serpent in The Garden. But that's just a laughable explanation. It isn't enough. How did that first caveman get the idea of putting his penis in a woman's mouth? Was it instinct? Was it a mistake? Was it libidinous visitors from another planet? WAS IT THE WOMAN'S IDEA? If it was the serpent it must have been some fucking serpent.

The sociologists say that it was animal instinct, but an altogether more convincing explanation is that it was the sheer boredom of having nothing to do – no TV, no game shows, no cooking-for-one books. That first caveman had more time on his hands, and on his penis. So he fooled around. For about two millenia. Today we reap the harvest of his idle hands and dirty thoughts.

CHAPTER 1

Your Body

We're all enlightened people, we live in a civilized society, we listen to the wisdom of our mothers, so we know that the way we look is precariously inconsistent and only a very small part of the way we actually are.

'It's not the packaging that counts, it's the present inside.' Okay, there's nothing wrong with this philosophy as a self-promotional technique, for those days when your scalp is flaking, spots are breaking out across your face and back, your stomach feels loose and caught up in the waistband of your trousers. On these days this cliché can be useful. However, on every other day, and indeed on about 90 per cent of ordinary occasions, it's complete bullshit.

If you're talking about love, about a communion of the spirit, about a lifetime together, then packaging isn't so important (although even the most highbrow of pristine romances generally starts with a bit of heavy petting). But if you're talking about something altogether more humble, if you're trying to touch someone's breasts rather than their soul, packaging and presentation is all-important. And packaging and presentation can be broken down into two main parts. Packaging your personality and your background (which we'll deal with in the next chapter), and grooming the product, which we'll deal with here.

An expert is called for. Let's go and ask the experts on all matters sexual – TEENAGERS – people who think about sex once every sixteen seconds.

SCENE: SUBURBAN LIVING ROOM, NIGHT

You can just about see it's the front room of an ordinary middle-class house. People are packed round the Queensway furniture, crammed between the Homebase wallpaper, despite the gloom many pairs of Raybanns nod coolly round the room. Bottles of cider, rum and Coke are packed onto the kitchen table, along with columns of paper cups. Wham! blazes from dad's stereo with a lot of V and heavy bass.

This is a TEENAGE PARTY.

A small group of males, red-label Levis, the odd earring, gelled hair, slight spraying of acne, are standing in one corner, gazing at a female group on the other side.

BOY 1: Kathy lets you, you know.
BOY 2: No, you're kidding.
BOY 1: She lets you.
BOY 2: You're kidding.
BOY 1: Well, she let me.
BOY 2: I wouldn't want to with Kathy.
BOY 1: Why?
BOY 2: She's a two.
BOY 1: She's a one.
BOY 2: I'm telling you, she's a two.
BOY 1: She may be a two but she does it like a one.
BOY 2: (looks unconvinced)
BOY 1: Well, at least she does it.
BOY 2: Look, she's great for a three like you or a four like Robbie, but not a one like me. I need a one. None of this two shit.
BOY 1: You're no one.
BOY 2: I'm a one, of course I'm a one. . . .

We slide between the heavily necking slow dancers, past the darkened orgy room which reverberates with the muffled sound of heavy petting, and insinuate ourselves among the teenagers.

VOICE OVER: I wonder whether you could just explain what makes someone a one, two, or three?
BOY 1: Oh, God, I mean you've got to be kidding, right?
VOICE OVER: No, actually.

And so they begin to explain the unwritten but rigorously applied physical sifting code by which teenagers from times prehistoric have worked out the level of their attractiveness. Every male in the West has come through a similar learning process, and although the terminology tends to differ, the principles are essentially the same. And while the sifting process is devised by teenagers, it stays largely the same throughout active heterosexual life.

The most recent labelling system to hit the teenage

Sex tip no. 2: Great Sexual Myths

Among the greatest sexually transmitted myths ever whispered over the secret fags behind the bike shed at school, greater even and more enduring than the 'what you can catch off the lavatory seat' series, is that concerning the origin of syphilis.

Long ago in the baked land of the ancient Pharaohs, runs the legend, the embalmers of the great and powerful were locked in their pyramids and given no contact with the outside world, except for the daily delivery of corpses.

As their sexual frustration grew over the years of isolation, beyond the soothing power even of frequent bursts of Ancient Egyptian masturbation (an art lost to man in the fifth century), they began to turn their attentions to the more beautiful of the female corpses left in their tombs. The heat, the decay, and the desperation produced syphilis which eventually broke out into the world with the escape of one trainee embalmer during the reign of King Tut 3. Complete bullshit, admittedly, but enough to hush the most arch of dinner parties.

---

party circuit is a sort of rough parody of the soccer league division tables, an analogy which actually works very well.

The points system was compiled by a group of twenty-five Girl Guides on one long night of objective passion seventeen years ago in a picturesque camping site in the Dordogne area of France. They provided the initial information. This was brought back to England by a Bromley schoolboy who gave it to his brother who expanded it at an early evening Ski Club reception and later a black tie reception at the home of a Venezuelan drugs runner.

The astonishing thing is that class and geography seem to have little effect on the physical grading of men. It all seems fairly instinctive. And yet not the 'I just can't explain why I like him' sort of instinctiveness. Girls seem to have an intimidatingly clear idea of which bits they find attractive in their men, and which bits they don't. ('Well, he's got super upper thighs, but his calves are a bit thin, and I wish his chest was a little broader. Also I don't like the way he's losing his hair. From the top rather than the side.')

Table 1

Minus points

Dry skin/pale skin:	−5
Receding hair:	−10
Spots on face:	−8
Spots on back:	−3
Spots on forehead:	−4

Spots need to be further qualified by type. An extra −2 points if they are deep red +2 points if they are faint and dried out.

Blackheads on nose:	−3
Red hair:	−5
Dandruff:	−4
Double chin:	−7
Big nose:	−7

Sticking-out ears: −6
Discoloured teeth: −5
Sticking-out teeth: −8
Lisp/speech defect: −8
Glasses: −4
Short (under 5′ 9″): −7
Big feet: −2
Fat: −9
Thin/weedy: −9
An enormous amount of bodily hair: −6
Visible moles/warts: −2 (for each one)
Asymetrical features: −5
Small/squinting eyes: −6
Rounded shoulders: −5
Hair on back: −5
Long nails: −5
Joined eyebrows: −6
Moustache: −3
Beards (under twenty-five): −4
Soft and fleshy hands: −5
High voice (unless you're Michael Jackson): −6
A strong regional accent: −2
American accent: −3

Positive points

Blond hair: +2
Good complexion: +5
A foreign accent: +6 (French/Italian an extra +2)
A soft regional accent: +5 (Scottish or Welsh an extra +2)
Firm, low voice: +5
Tan: +8
Good teeth: +5
Strong colour eyes: +8 (an extra +4 for green or blue eyes)
Long eyelashes: +4
Chiselled nose: +5
Tall (5′ 9″ or over): +7

Good body:	+6
Quite a good body:	+5
This can be further broken as follows:	
Very little hair on legs:	+5
Flat stomach:	+7
Good legs:	+6
Good bottom:	+7
Well-groomed hair:	+4
Five o'clock shadow:	+4
	(unless it's red, then −2)
Hard hands:	+5
Being famous:	+8
Being rich:	+10

The table works very simply. You start with 25 points and then add or subtract according to the items listed. Your final scores are graded as follows:

50+: premier league
35+: first division
25+: second division
15+: third division

Anything below – fourth division or non-league.

Using the table

You have to begin by taking off your clothes, taking a long deep breath, and staring at yourself, hard, in the mirror. In daylight. Don't try and lie to yourself. Gaze as objectively as you can at the physical specimen in front of you, in much the same way as you would look at a woman lying on a beach through mirrored sunglasses. Add up your score and isolate your weaknesses.

The key here is not to get too depressed if you're coming out with a very low score and a low league ranking.

First, there are many other factors we are yet to discuss which can alter your league division standing – the way you smell, what you say, where you live, how much you earn. You get the picture.

Second, the great thing about the league is the concept of the good cup run.

A third-division side should basically not do too well in the course of a whole season, in the routine, week-in, week-out matches. But it can pull off occasional quite astonishing victories over much higher-ranked teams in the cup competitions. Division 3 men often get off with Division 1 women, beating even premier league teams into submission. So don't be unnerved.

Sex tip no. 3: Statistics

Everyone knows statistics lie like a politician or a man with his penis in a girl's mouth, but there is one statistic, often quoted, which needs to be exposed for the half-truth it is. You'll often hear that you don't need to worry about your looks, your clothes, your personality, about carefully choosing the girl you're going to ask out, because statistics are on your side. A man, the statistical myth runs, stood on the steps of the National Gallery in London and asked the first one hundred women that he saw whether they would go to bed with him. Ninety-nine said no. But one said yes. Which is true. But what's never told is that the researcher was so messed up, lacking in confidence and confused by ninety-nine consecutive rejections that by the time the Law of Averages came to his rescue he didn't want sex. He asked number one hundred to come home and throw pickled artichokes at his bottom. Use the league tables. They'll help you.

Working on Your Weaknesses

Going bald

It would be far better not to be going bald. There's no use pretending otherwise, it's a real drag. Unlike a tan, a Porsche, or aquamarine eyes, baldness is not considered by most women to be inherently attractive. Forget Telly Savalas, forget Jack Nicholson, forget Yul Brynner, forget Clint Eastwood. Their receding hairlines are made up for by their box office receipts and their taste-melting international fame.

Baldness is bad.

We know both from Hollywood and our own childhoods that baldness isn't a good thing. Everyone has had that terrible experience at the age of about thirteen when body consciousness is dawning, and someone at the school bus stop tells you that they can see a bald patch on the back of your head. You laugh it off but four days later you're still going into your mother's bedroom taking her hand mirror and bending over backwards in front of the main mirror trying to spot where the patch begins. And in Hollywood they know baldness isn't a good thing because no one on 'Dynasty' is losing their hair. Not even elderly Blake. In LA young stars now insure themselves against hair loss!

I mean let's face it. Baldness being primarily a hereditary thing, were the affliction that terrible the unfortunate victims wouldn't be allowed to mate and perpetuate their species. They'd be left to die out, single, alone, shunned, a genetic mutation spurned by the healthy and hirsute. As it is, one in three men are thinning, AND THEY'RE STILL GETTING OFF WITH GIRLS. History has seen hundreds of square miles of male scalp bared by retreating hairlines, with very little diminution of the more exposed owners' ability to find girls.

While it's not a plus to be losing your hair, it's not the ultimate minus. For instance, it's not nearly as bad as smelling.

It's all a question of attitude.

Forget wigs, forget hair weaving, forget hair salon disguises. Don't linger over those ads in the evening papers otherwise you begin to feel like some hated member of a persecuted minority, apologetically going up the Underground escalators trying to look at the 'baldness cured' posters without anyone seeing. Your attitude must be aggressive, unembarrassed, not defensive and awkward. Elton John came to be regarded as a bald man when in fact he was only quite a bald man, because he tried so hard to prevent it. Bobby Charlton became more bald than he actually was by scraping his hopelessly thin line of hair over his shiny scalp in an increasingly futile attempt to hide it. Grow your hair longer and thicker at the back, part it into the bald patch if it's receding from the side, gel your hair back if it's receding from the front. Don't acknowledge it as a crippling weakness and girls won't either. Above all try and avoid the hackneyed technique of coping with less hair by chopping off what remains until flat and slightly spiked and then trying to balance it out by growing a thin, prickly beard to make up for the lack of hair on top. This screams, 'I've got a problem with my hair loss' even louder than a cheap wig.

Let the hair that's left grow thicker and longer, and have it cut more imaginatively. Have it coloured or twisted, make it a trademark, not a pockmark. And remember baldness does also have its advantages. As a hairline recedes so does the dandruff-infected scalp acreage. Also, in the sun, men with less hair come away looking much browner because they have so much more tannable skin to display the new colour on. They also look far better in sunglasses, for some so far unexplained reason.

Eyes

Everyone, even the most inexperienced lover, knows that eyes are important. You can tell because so many songs are written about them. And the extraordinary thing about eyes is that for things that small they can look so bad.

How can such a small area of white look so horrendously red after what macho types call 'a hard night'? Given that you've got a fairly good pair of eyes (i.e. two of them), what can you do to make them better? Well, this is tough. First there's contact lenses, tinted ones. Blue eyes do have a certain cachet, and tinted lenses can seem like a good answer. Except that they tend to make them too blue, a sort of electric aquamarine blue, which gives you a rather glazed-over, vacant look. It might be described as Zombie Flesh-Eater's George Peppard. This isn't desirable. So what else is there? Well, you can also dye your eyelashes. This is an excruciatingly embarrassing thing to ask for, but once done makes a quite astonishing difference, as long as the colour is matched well. If it's slapped on too dark you go all *Clockwork Orange* which frightens people off, or too *Cabaret*, which means you get beaten up for being a poof. Probably the best current answer, to be taken fast while the trend still lasts, is dark glasses.

Spots

Face spots are undoubtedly serious handicaps in the pursuit of women, but however large, festering and ingrown they may appear, the majority do clear up in the late teens. The agonizing reality for many men, however, is that just about the time their faces clear up their hair starts receding. The range of miracle potions available now almost matches those for foot fungi (no mean feat since in terms of sales athlete's foot remains one of the developed world's most passionate preoccupations). Treat your spots as much as you want, although teenage experience tends to suggest that the best treatment is no treatment, apart from sunlight. Slap on the potions that clean the spots and cover them with skin colour cosmetic at the same time. That satisfies the neurosis and appeases the pores simultaneously.

Spots on the back are altogether more complicated. Of course because they are hidden they seem to be less immediately important. But the moment you're successful with a woman they can have a major impact. She's going to start pushing her hands up your shirt, trying to unbutton it, and start taking it off. The obvious solution is to keep the shirt on, or at least slip a T-shirt on while getting into bed. But the problem with back spots is that they're normally rather large which means they can be easily felt. And you can't *really* stop your partner from taking your T-shirt off. You will, after all, have been rampaging through her clothing and whether you started at the top or the bottom you will sooner or later be laying your hands on one sexual target or other. Most girls will want to participate, too, but their choices are very limited. Unbuttoning a man's trousers is considered really a bit forward unless they've been dating for quite a while. It's going straight for the principal target. Shirts on the other hand provide access to the back, chest and shoulders which, while being neutral, are not entirely insensitive. This way the girl can feel involved too. A shirts-on rule can thus be a difficult one to enforce. However if the spots persist after you've tried changing your sheets more often, changing your shirts more often, and getting it out in the open more often, you're probably going to have to stick to the no-shirt-off policy and just hope.

Sex tip no. 4: Nails

It's so easy to forget to cut your nails, but you always must make sure to do it on the evening of a date. The problem is that they're so easy to forget until you're actually in bed with your fingers about to go nomad hunting.

Suddenly you feel them catch on something. The whole thing's so sensitive down there that she'll be able to tell exactly how each one is within about ½mm. This is as bad as dandruff. CUT THEM.

Exercising your body/Dieting

In the original *Star Trek* movie we were treated to a rare insight into the way the Galactic Federation trains its future Starship captains. They have to deal with a simulated hyperspace confrontation in which there is no obvious way to win. A space ship is crippled in neutral territory, it's sending out a mayday signal. Klingon ships are in the vicinity, and if the Starship cadet responds to the call he might provoke an attack, and start a war. If he doesn't respond the distressed ship is going to blow up with all its crew. Captain James T. Kirk (everyone's favourite) nicknamed this 'a no-win situation'.

Such 'no-win' situations also occur in the greater and altogether more dangerous pursuit of women. One such 'no-win' situation was reported by a twenty-six-year-old investment banker. His body tended to be naturally flabby. He knew this held him back with women so he decided to undertake a rigorous programme of physical exercise. He would swim one day, and go to the gym the next. His body responded well, so did the girls. His shoulders broadened, his stomach flattened, his confidence soared. But unfortunately the daily showers which followed the exercise accelerated his hair loss.

What could he do?

He had to choose between a firm, muscular body, and a full head of hair. He chose the body.

This was the right choice in a tough situation. Hair is very important to girls, but bodies are generally more so. Both is better, but there is a definite difference in sex-appeal values.

Now when considering a programme of exercise from the point of view of catching girls you need to distinguish between health and fitness, and looks. We are not concerned with health or fitness. This is cosmetic fitness. Finding the fastest way to look better, more attractive. Steve Ovett is fit and healthy, but can you hold your hand on your heart and say you really want to look like he does?

Obviously not. Forget lungs and heart, the trimmest vital organ in the world isn't going to pull you the loneliest woman in the nightclub. The vital areas are the shoulders, stomach and bottom. Clothes hang best when these are in good shape. Tell this to the trainer in the gym. He'll work you out. Even more effective than lifting weights and doing circuits is swimming. This pulls everything in tight but done regularly has the added bonus of giving hair a slightly golden tint, as the chlorine strips the protein from your follicles. This allows you to carry your athletic credibility with you everywhere, rather than just when you wear your tracksuit.

Sex tip no. 5: Calling a New Girlfriend by the Old One's Name

This is a dreadful thing to do. The problem is that it's so easy. If you've spent quite a while with one girlfriend, have got a special nickname for her, especially if she's lived with you or spent a lot of time around your flat or house, it's so easy to let her name slip out to a new girl. The results can be terrible. It hurts like sin, and generally provokes a deeply emotional or incensed response.

There's only one way out. You have to get straight into a holding hands, having a long chat and deep hug position with her on the couch and then start explaining that the only reason you did it was because she has already come to mean so much to you. You've been with her just a matter of weeks and already you feel so natural around her that the old name came out, the name of a girl you virtually lived with for months. It's a testimony to how much she already means to you, not of how she's just a replacement.

If you've been going out with her longer than you did the old one, or at least have told her that the old one wasn't important then you're simply in trouble.

Gyms/Health Clubs

The way women look, and the methods they use to make themselves look better, and the way men look and the methods they use to make themselves look better, lie at the very heart of the gulf between the sexes, and all the new problems which have sprung from it. Before the man, standing in front of his mirror, assessing his score from the tables, ventures into the health clubs, the diet books and the hair salon intent on promotion he has to understand the fundamental difference, and the fundamental injustice which makes everything so hard.

Okay, there was a time when it was really hard for women. Actually, a very long time. Men worked, women didn't, men were defined by their work, women were defined by their looks. Ugly girls had to try and patch something together or else they languished on the shelf or the wall paper. This was bad news and unfair.

But at least the ugly girls, like all the other girls, were allowed to try and make themselves look better. They could look at themselves in mirrors in public, they could put make-up on in public, they could be girls, and no one thought any the less of them for trying. They were fulfilling their duties as women.

Then came sexual equality. A good thing. Women could still make themselves look pretty, but they could also compete for the jobs and the status that came with them.

So what did the men do? Answer: They got fucked up. Women were now defined by how they looked, and how they worked. Men just by how they worked. And they weren't working as much. Women were doing it better, being paid more.

Men got all confused. Women looked great. They looked at themselves in mirrors in public. They had highly paid jobs.

Men still looked bad, didn't dare look in the mirror in public, and they couldn't even pull rank by their jobs.

They had to learn how to look good too. They had to

invade some part of the female domain to be able to compete, or just plain keep up. But it was so hard. Women could work, and it was no problem going to health clubs, lying on the sunbed, taking an overt unembarrassed concern in their appearance because they'd always been allowed to.

But men couldn't. They'd been the macho ones. They'd been the ones that had always been manly. They had to look like men, but not be seen to care about it, certainly not be seen to do anything about it. Health clubs for men are a complete fiction when they're billed as sanctions, retreats, saviours of the male body. They are terrifying places, dominated by body beautifuls who would pull women all the time even if they didn't work out. They stalk around gyms, sneering at wrinkled, flabby, normal men, doing their best, embarrassed to the point of tears (far more pain from this than the physical ardour).

You see, take one third-division man, and one third-division woman. It's so much easier for the woman. Say they both have the same job – travel agents – and they both have the same looks. The girl's way ahead. She'll lie on a sunbed, have highlights in her hair, make-up on, the whole works. The man will be down because he doesn't have a job which makes him more special (women still have kudos just by doing a job), and he finds it far more difficult to lie on the sunbed, work out, have his hair highlighted, all the things that would lift him to her level, because it's embarrassing to be a man and ask for these things. Result, she goes up a division, he stays put and gets depressed. And depression leads to relegation.

The horror of the gym

And gyms can be tough in many other ways too. Everyone's acquainted with the pattest of all pat pieces of philosophy, 'There's always someone who's better looking, more intelligent, wealthier, sharper and more amusing than you are.' Well, you'll find them all at the gym. The result is that gyms can be profoundly depressing places. Good-looking people burst from every corner, as do mirrors, just to heighten your anguish. You will notice that these gym regulars are completely unabashed when it comes to looking in mirrors, blow-drying their hair, using the sunbeds, or putting on moisturiser after they've showered. Bullies and the very good-looking are never afraid of being called wimps. It's only those average types who make up 99 per cent of the population who slink in with a moderate paunch, slight spray of back spots, slightly receding hair, and not quite sure where the lavatories are that have the problem. There's really no answer to this one. Try and use the gym at off-peak times, avoid the celebrities and body beautifuls (this means going mid-morning, mid-afternoon, or very early at the weekends), and never, absolutely never, attempt to pick up a woman inside, particularly the ones working at the reception desk.

These girls will always be good-looking and extremely friendly, but you have to cultivate an attitude towards those who work in your gym of icy distance. They are privvy to your most intimate physical faults, and your most embarrassing physical goals. Be friendly but keep them at arm's length. A failed attempt at asking one out will probably involve you having to join a new club. Possibly moving to a different part of town.

Sunbeds

These are extremely useful. Often they won't make you look brown but they do give you a healthy, fresh-faced sort of glow. The only drawback is that you can't really afford to let other people know you use them. So don't use them more than twice a week, this will stop it being too obvious. Then, providing you go for the occasional run (or at least sit around your flat looking like you might just have been for one), you can always put the flush in your complexion down to the wind, or the weather. 'Wind tan' is a very good phrase to have associated with yourself. When you've found yourself in the gym with no one else there and a sunbed open, sneak in, even if you haven't got a booking, and have a good look at how it works. The key to not making sunbed use massively embarrassing is to make it look as calm, confident and practised as possible. On your first booking you don't want to be fumbling around with the controls, having to go out into the locker room and ask one of the weight lifters if they know how it operates. You need to be able to walk straight in, drop in your token and go to it immediately. The less fuss you make, the less you will be noticed. This should be learnt as a general rule and applied to all activities which it would be embarrassing to be caught doing wrongly (apart from masturbation which it is embarrassing to be caught doing wrongly or rightly).

Food and diets

All forms of exercise are good ways of losing weight, but none as effective as cutting down on your food. The problem for the ambitious male is how to market the fact that he is on a diet. Because being on a diet is virtually to admit that you have a weight problem, and having a weight problem is another one of those inherently unattractive things like baldness, spots and smallness. So you have to find a way of marketing it. This is extremely important because so many dates and opportunities with girls revolve around food. If you're forever turning down puddings, salad dressings, and consulting calorie sheets, you're gradually chipping away at your sexual credibility. The fact is that it is okay for a girl to be on a diet, but generally not okay for a male.

So what do you do?

The answer is in fact simple. You just have to pick the right sort of dietary image. Calorie-conscious diets are terrible. Calorie-conscious diets dressed up as health-conscious diets are not. Naturally you have to avoid the crankier extremes (the vegan diet, for instance, isn't considered a great aphrodisiac) but making a point of avoiding red meat (cholesterol), staying away from fatty oily foods (heart disease), and rarely eating highly sugared puddings (tooth decay), when mixed in with dashes of athleticism and a slightly sporty look, deceive most observers completely. They'll never guess you're trying to lose weight.

The Boy George phenomenon

The gender-bending phenomenon has confused a lot of men in the past few years. It's a difficult concept to grasp. Why should a man who is prettier than most of the women actually be able to pick up more of them than his more standardly macho rivals? Well, the first part of the answer is fairly easy. The really successful gender-benders also happened to be fantastically wealthy and famous rock stars. This did work in their favour. However, for a while it did look as though everyone was going to rush into lip gloss and mascara. But fortunately the return of Marilyn to the male fold, the eclipsing of Boy George, and the disappearance of Michael Jackson has whittled away at the rage for feminine men. Duran Duran and Wham! are undeniably pretty boys, but they are at least boys. This does make things easier for the fashion-conscious male. Make-up isn't easy stuff to deal with and you can almost guarantee that the night you have your hair set, your eyes lined, and your lips glossed, will be the night it pours with rain or you get caught outside the off-licence by the local skinheads. The safest techniques are eyelash dying, face-pack spot treatments, and sunbeds because no one ever knows.

Clothes

Everyone has their own style and each date has its own tone so there aren't really any cast-iron rules about what you should and shouldn't wear as long as you stay away from the most violent stylistic clichés (cowboy boots and jeans with big buckled belts, tracksuit trousers tucked into white socks, leather ties with piano keys marked on them). If you can also stay away from the more adventurous of modern man's synthetic fibre creations (anything which sounds more like kitchen tiling than fashion styling) then you'll be on even safer ground. Even if it means having a smaller wardrobe. It's better to have two sets which won't melt when you're standing near the radiator than five that will.

The only real rules which need to be observed are those relating to disguise. Stripes and colours can radically affect the way your body looks. For instance if you have small rounded shoulders you must avoid shirts that have hoops or vertical lines boldly marked around the shoulder area. Keep the lines and markings horizontal to make you look broader. The opposite applies to waistlines. Horizontal stripes make you look fatter, vertical ones suck you in and make you look taller.

If you're uncertain about what colour combinations to wear on the night of a date, play it safe. You get no points, and generally no sex, for violent near-misses. When you're going out at night always wear something which is comfortable enough to run in in the event of an emergency, and also loose enough to avoid widespread sighting of any erections you may get in the course of the evening. If the

---

Sex tip no. 6: Combating sexual guilt

The moment you feel yourself starting to feel guilty about what is beginning to flit through your mind, pause for a moment and run over a list of the great figures in history who have also had the same dirty thoughts. Don't sniff or feel embarrassed about wanting to touch someone's breasts, because some of the most significant affairs in history have started with heavy petting. Dennis Thatcher, Winston Churchill, Romeo, Hitler, Ronald Reagan, Lech Walecsza, Franz Kafka, Albert Einstein, you name them, they've all at some point in their lives thought 'Men Only' fantasies, and lavished their history-shaping attention on a simple breast or button.

---

trousers are on the tight side make sure they have deep pockets so that the moment you feel an erection stirring you can plunge in your hand and disguise the growing lump.

Mirrors

Mirrors are very important, but you have to understand that they never tell the same story. The mirror in the bathroom can make you look unbelievably good, and the mirror in the hall can make you look unrealistically bad. It's best to try and have a spread of mirrors in your house. Artificial light is softer and often makes you look like you've got muscles and an outline that you actually don't have. Daylight is far harsher but can wash out the effect of really quite bad spots. The best mirrors are those which give you enough room to stand a fairly long way back. This lets you start off being too far away to look really bad and then move in gradually until you've reached your optimum distance. When you're feeling unattractive and know you're in trouble, don't rush into the bad mirrors. This is stupid. Stay with the good mirror, or just ignore mirrors altogether. This was Mae West's technique and it never failed her.

The Size of Your Penis

This is it. The prime concern. The ultimate worry. The evergreen male fascination. How large am I compared to the others? It's a funny business this because men spend a lot of time, relatively speaking, in the company of other nude men. Just think of all those changing room years at school, and matches down at the local club. Obviously nobody goes around checking things out too closely, there's always the terrible fear of being caught looking too long and being thought a homosexual, a child molester, or worse. Nevertheless, most men are interested and do take a peek at the penis action that comes their way. The average man can expect to see far more naked men in the course of his life than the average woman. In fact the chances are that he'll see far more naked men than he will naked women. But he hardly ever sees an erect penis – apart from his own, that is.

No big deal on the surface this, though it illustrates the fundamental point that men are mortified by their erections at the same time as being turned on by them (it's nice when a sympathetic girl looks at it, but terrible if one of your friends sees it). The result is that though every man comes with a complete set of jokes about small penises, medium-sized penises, and massively over-sized penises, he doesn't really know what 'small', 'medium', or 'large' are in penis terms.

Let's clear this up.

It's not how large it is, it's what you do with it. This is another one of those clichés which sound horribly wooden, and a little bit hollow. In fact it is largely true when you're talking about the size of a man's member. As long as you're a fairly normal size there's really no problem. It is a matter not of a few extra inches, but a few extra moves. Technique really is all. But we need a benchmark to work out exactly where normal stops and small starts. It's difficult to tell exactly because women tend to be in a fairly intense state of arousal when they've got to the point of seeing the penis which has been lying in wait for them, which means it's quite hard to be completely accurate. Most, however, say that if in an erect state you're not much larger than the length of your extended little finger, then you're pretty small.

So, for the record:

Small is 3½″ or less, fully erect.
Medium is 4″ to 6″ fully erect.
Large is 6 to 7½″, fully erect.
Extra large is anything over.

So what happens if you've stopped for a few moments to check yourself out and find that you're in the small category? Well, it's like everything else, baldness, spots, fat, being small isn't considered an attractive asset but that's the way it is. Stop worrying about it and trying to pretend you're not as small as you actually are. You're small. Get over the tears and the protestations. Given that you're small you are going to have to be more imaginative when it comes to foreplay and all the other bits and pieces which make up sex. This is rare so get a reputation for being good at it (it's often far more important and a lot more fun than the penetration stuff anyway). And second, women are all different depths themselves anyway. Some are much smaller than others. It's just a matter of time before you find someone who's just the right shape for you. A last-minute addition here. Forget the ads in the back of the men's magazines about penis enlargement. The magazines themselves can be far more helpful in this respect. There is some circumstantial evidence to suggest that masturbation can make the penis get bigger. There probably won't be anything too dramatic, but what a pleasant form of working out. It's worth a try even if there's only a faint chance of success.

CHAPTER 2

Your Personality

Looks are terribly important. In the sexual game they are, if you like, the product. But your personality, the way you choose to introduce the details of your background, your job, your goals, these make up the marketing. And as anyone who has ever watched a soap-on-the rope rot for months in the clutter at the back edge of the bath will know, a completely hopeless product, with the right marketing, can achieve widespread sales. This marketing is often the key to the good cup runs that we mentioned earlier.

There are no rights or wrongs when it comes to personalities that appeal to girls, just effective and ineffective. Effective personalities move smoothly, with a dash of mystery, two dashes of sensitivity, a twirl of bravado, a sugaring of boyishness or alternatively of manliness, and a slight suggestion of vulnerability. This formula serves as a character outline for every major Hollywood lead for the past forty years. Ineffective personalities move in a series of kangaroo hops, their clutches are always let out too early. They are moody, bitter, invariably depressed, and afraid.

But the first thing to understand is that you don't actually have to be attractive to pick up a girl. You just have to appear attractive.

So you don't need to worry about trying to change your personality, just presenting it in its most attractive light. This generally means scaling up or down from what you naturally are. For instance if you generally feel paralysed with embarrassment in the company of women, and therefore spend long evenings without saying a word, try and present your saying nothing in a slightly darker more mysterious manner. Don't look nervous, and if you can only speak falteringly don't do it. But when you say nothing, make it look like what you're not saying would really be worth listening to.

Wrong way of saying nothing

GIRL: You're not saying much.
NERVOUS GUY: Yes, it's well, I suppose, huh . . .
GIRL: Do you know anyone here?
NERVOUS GUY: Oh, hardly anyone, I mean, just one or two, huh . . .
GIRL: Do you live around here?
NERVOUS GUY: No, actually, wish I did, huh . . .
GIRL: See you later.

Right way of saying nothing

GIRL: You're not saying much.
GUY (*enigmatic smile*): I know.
GIRL: Do you know anyone here?
GUY: Some.
GIRL: Do you live round here?
GUY: You're kidding.
GIRL: Could I see you later?

If on the other hand you're very highly strung, indiscreet, and generally the sort of person who is told to shut up, scale it down slightly to an energetic, life-and-soul-of-the-party image, rather than the full-bodied pain in the neck.

The area of your personality that you have most control over is your job and career goals. What you do for a living and what you want to do for a living are both crucial considerations in a girl's mind when she's considering whether she is going to let you put your tongue in her mouth. Certain professions are not obvious points winners, yet any job, however tedious it sounds, or actually is, can be improved on immeasurably by a little dressing up. Consider accounting. The City has become much more glamorous since all the dramatic takeovers and hostile bids, the Dallas-style fighting, the money, the intrigue and its James Bond in pinstripes. See if you have a job description which is dull and introduce it in a more detailed way.

Wrong

GIRL: Hi, I've been watching you all evening. What do you do?
GUY: I'm an accountant.
GIRL: Is that the time?

Right

GIRL: Hi, I've been watching you all evening. What do you do?
GUY: I'm kind of a financial detective, I investigate companies' finances. *Or*: I work in the City.
GIRL: Is that the time? Would you walk me home?

Almost any job is susceptible to this sort of tinkering. A plumber might introduce himself as a domestic troubleshooter, a builder would try and tie in the roles of contractor and architect ('I put up skyscrapers'), window cleaners are 'steeple jacks', electricians are in 'electronics', draughtsmen are 'industrial artists', journalists '*write* for the *Daily Express*', clerks are 'administrative assistants' or 'personal assistants'. And anyone who isn't sure is simply 'in business'.

The thing about this sort of marketing is that it doesn't matter how patently false it may appear as soon as the girl gets to know you better because it only has to work for that crucial initial impression stage. Providing you get your foot in the door early on and give her a chance to inspect the goods rather than dismissing them on the basis of the label, it's serving its function. And it's good to appear to

Sex tip no. 7: Space Sex

One question that's often asked by inquisitive men is, 'Did the astronauts get randy?' and 'Were they able to have erections in zero gravity?' And this is an important one should the future of our species ever come to depend on a flight from Earth into deep space. Forget the lasers and computers – if we can't take a few erections with us we're goners. Well, the answer is intriguing.

Having the 'Right Stuff' didn't necessarily mean being a super macho lover, virtually an erection with wings. No, sir. However, the lads that went up were naturally quite tough, pretty fit, and liable to the occasionable dirty thought, even that high up with so many more elevated things on their minds. And the extraordinary thing about zero gravity erections was

THEY DIDN'T ALWAYS GO UP!!

Can you imagine an erection pointing sideways? OR STRAIGHT DOWN?

But that was just the beginning of the fun. Do you think all those men, tough, military, drinking, driving, red-blooded heroes didn't want to mess about a bit, have a laugh? Okay 'the first man to walk on the moon' as a title was already gone, but what about 'the first man to come in space', or 'the first man to wank on the moon'? So they never told us officially that these jock experiments were going on, but can you really believe that the lunar module never once got sprayed by an over-enthusiastic erection? And imagine the problems with clearing up. Often you'd have to grab your Kleenex and run around after the released sperm, swiping at it.

What an adventure!

---

have goals or ambitions. Girls assess men far more materially than men do women – if we are clothes strippers, they are asset strippers. A man with prospects is a considerable turn-on – a man with no idea (unless he is terribly successful or in a job most would kill for) is losing points. What's really being said here is that a great-looking girl is a great-looking girl no matter what job she does. She could be in the insect extermination business and men would still pursue her. A man, however, despite sexual equality, remains far more strongly identified with his job. No bug exterminator, however good-looking, is going to be really first division.

So, here are another set of career points which can be added or subtracted from your previous score.

Table 2

Accounting:	−5
Architecture:	+3
Doctor:	+4
Driving instructor:	−3
Stockbroker:	−1
Plumber (everyone wants a plumber as a friend):	+3
Electrician (everyone wants an electrician as a friend):	+2
Banker:	−1
Journalist:	+1
Publishing:	+3
Anything to do with movies (the only drawback being that they are largely gay, neurotic, or have AIDS):	+7
Artist:	+4
Teacher:	−1
Model:	+5
Tennis pro:	+6
Any exec on an expense account (apart from pet food or toys – when it's −2):	+2
Optician:	level par
Hairdresser:	+4

Dentist:	+3
Anything to do with airlines:	+4
All other travel business:	+3
Anything to do with sports:	+4
Anything to do with fashion:	+4
Anyone running their own business:	+4
Anything to do with filing:	−2
Butcher:	−1
DHSS inspector:	−3
Social worker:	−2
Chemist:	level par
Drug pushers:	−3
Anyone working at the DVLC at Swansea:	−5
Store detectives:	−2
Traffic wardens:	−2
Glamour photographers: (unless you've got a title, then +2)	−1
Gardeners:	−1
Farmers:	−1
Politicians:	−2
Market researchers:	−2

Cars

Cars, like jobs, remain things with which men are heavily identified, far more heavily identified than women. A woman in a Robin Reliant is interesting. A guy in a Reliant is a wimp.

If you've got a less than dramatic car customize it a little, or beat it up a little, certainly don't ride it around as if you're happy to have it just as it is. Make out that you've got it because it's so different, an anti-status symbol, a piece of inverted snobbery, or because you just don't give a damn what you drive.

Not having a car can be something of a blow, especially if you can't afford taxis, even more if she's got a car. If she does, don't let her take it with you as a passenger, to the date destination. This puts you in too much of a submissive position, from which it's hard to lead. It's like being ferried round by someone's older brother or sister. Have her leave her car at your place or wherever you arranged to meet, and then go on and back by taxi or public transport. On *your* tab. This at least gives you the moral lead.

There is a way of turning a no-car situation to your advantage with certain sorts of women. Some girls quite like slightly mothering men. It's touch and go because, a bit like 'just good friends' relationships, they do tend to have their less passionate side. However, the passion is far less elusive than in the friends version. It sort of spills into the older women/Joan Collins/let me show you how, style of sex. This is great providing you are boyish looking, enthusiastic, and don't have too obvious a five o'clock shadow. In this event use her car all the time. She'll love it.

Renting fast cars

This is a date which has become more popular recently. Hiring a very fast car for the day, and then taking the girl for a cruise. Obviously an amazing car is tremendously impressive. They also tend to have laid-back, low-slung seats which can be a great help when it comes to pass time (unless they're the ultra-sporty, scooped-out bucket seats which are virtually impossible to get out of). However, the real drawback is that high-performance cars are designed for high-performance driving – they really don't work that well at speeds of under 40 m.p.h., and hardly at all in first or second gear. This means that if you start going up over the BMW range you're going to run into serious kangaroo hop trouble as you try and cruise gently up the King's Road. And as with all things that draw attention to yourself, it hurts a lot more if you fuck up because it's so much more public. Nobody cares if you stall in a beaten-up old Morris. Do it with a girl beside you in a Ferrari in the middle of the Saturday High Street rush and you're going to end up in tears and stood up.

Are Porsches sexy?

There's been far too much rubbish talked about this lately.

There is admittedly a white sock, fake tan and gold chain element which has snapped up large parts of the second-hand Porsche market, and spivvy isn't the turn-on it once was. However, they have tended to confine their attentions to the 928 and 944 series. 911 series remain extremely seductive cars. And even though 928s and 944s may not be what they once were, and sure Mel Gibson or Paul Newman in a Honda Civic would certainly pull all the women they wanted, the average guy will attract a lot more attention in a Porsche than a Honda. There's no two ways about it. Spivvy, yes. Sexy, definitely.

Sex tip no. 8: Age

Men generally start lying about their age seriously (to lie seriously about your age means pretending to be younger than you really are, not older) at about the same age as women. Around the twenty-five mark. It's a sensitive time. You really are beginning to leave the ranks of 'young people', to become 'people'. You can't have a railcard, your car insurance costs less, your friends are getting married. It's the age when bits start falling off your body – hair, teeth, you get the odd wrinkle.

This can be depressing. But it's less depressing for males than for females. It's one of the biggest teenage clichés that girls always go for older guys. At fifteen this is a real pain in the neck, eighteen, nineteen and twenty-year-olds are grabbing everything that's really nice, and you're lucky to find a girl left over who isn't twelve or under. However, the balance does gradually swing back in the male's favour. Things get a little easier as you go through your late teens and early twenties, the supply of available younger girls seeming to get bigger, and your inhibitions about their age receding. Then, as you hit the twenty-five mark, the balance takes a big lurch in the males' favour. By this age the single woman has passed the optimum age for her first marriage and first child, and, very slightly they start to panic. You can see it in their eyes and their highlights. This opens up the field a little, giving you a shot at contemporaries as well as the youth market. Into your thirties and the divorcée market opens up, the youth market remaining a respectable alternative until approximately thirty-five, after which it starts to get a little seedy. The forties remain divorcées and occasional married affairs, until the dramatic swing back of the fifties when the male is grabbed by the male menopause, squeezes back into his size 34 red label Levis and heads for the school gates. He ridicules himself for the last seven years of strong sexual activity while older women look on and giggle under their breath.

It is a fact that 'bachelor' sounds better than 'spinster'; men do retain their looks longer, and therefore have more time, but remember that the term 'confirmed bachelor' takes over at around forty, the tabloid euphemism for 'gay'. You really have to be very publically heterosexual to overwhelm the implied 'confirmed' status. The only heterosexual alternative to 'bachelor' is 'playboy' which frankly starts sounding stupid once the middle-age spread sets in.

CHAPTER 3

Finding Girls

One of the many Sod's laws of sex relates to the non-availability of women. It's a fact that at discos or parties when you have no girl with you, there seems to be no women who are either available, or if they are, the slightest bit interested in you. But the moment you have persuaded one to dance, the walls will seem to be packed with girls making eyes.

The moment you're alone again, they will all have disappeared. Statistics provide a profoundly unsatisfying answer to this recurrent, frustrating problem. According to the figures there are far more single women than men – the simple fact that they live longer than men should mean the supply of females is ample, even if it's only in the old people's homes.

But statistics lie.

There is always a shortage of women, just like there is always a shortage of cabs when it's raining. And the reason seems to be something to do with the strength of the male sex drive. An immensely popular, and almost unbelievably sexually experienced tennis-pro at a resort near Marbella describes the moment this profound truth manifested itself to him last summer in a voice of tremulous awe. . . . 'I'd been working in resorts for eight years straight, sleeping with an average of one woman every ten days, and watching men pursuing them and asking for advice all around me. Suddenly it hit me. The overriding purpose of the majority of men's lives could be summed up in one phrase: men just want to fuck models.'

This may sound simplistic at first but in fact it is a profound truth, a truth which sinks in the more it is considered. Men spend their entire lives chasing women, trying to impress them, worrying about how they appear to them, evaluating themselves by their ability to go out with them. And the better looking the girl, the greater the satisfaction the man feels. Women tend to be different. Sex and men are of course important, but generally they are not the lifelong, overriding concerns that they are to men. Because of this, because men want to do it more than women, men are destined always to be looking, searching and competing. Women will always be making the choices.

Only in New York and your dreams will women fall continually into your lap.

So how do you find them?

When you suddenly get an overpowering urge to find a woman, and TV, food, or those letters you should have written won't take it off your mind, you need to relax. Women-hungry men tend to veer between desperate highs and equally desperate lows, depending on the immediate availability of girls. The laws state that the lows start when they have gone out looking for girls, failed to find any, and then sat around at home for hours, intermittently masturbating, scanning the 'TV Times' for programmes that might show some nudity, and eating. Okay, the key is to relax. Get ready slowly, have a bath or a shower, and consider how many women you see in shops, on buses, in trains, at the office every day. They are not the wilful princesses imprisoned in suburban towers that they sometimes seem when you're desperately looking for them. A good way to start is to write down the name of every girl you know, single or not. Each one will know at least twenty other girls, who will each know twenty more. Suddenly the female population won't seem so tantalizingly out of reach.

But where do you go for them?

There are two main schools of thought. First there's the daylight school, those who prefer finding women in ordinary, daily situations, at bus stops, in shops, in restaurants, at the office.

Then there are the nightlifers, those who go straight to clubs or places which are designed specifically for picking up girls, thinly disguised as bars, cafés or discos. Many singles cultures are rapidly changing from the nightlife concept to the daylight one. Take Southern California, the original home of the singles bar. The supermarket pick-up was the craze of last year, a crude technique which involved making signals with your trolley to female shoppers, and if they were well received, making the date in the queue at the till. Most recently they have discovered the Freeway singles club, a 1200-strong membership which slaps secret stickers on the number plates of its cars, identifying them as single and interested to other members of the club who happen to drive down the same bit of road. They can then check each other out at the next jam, or at the next traffic lights.

But how do you do it?

Finding women really isn't a problem. Just spend a morning noticing how many women you actually meet in a normal day, waitresses, fellow commuters, sales assistants, scores of them. The first thing to get used to is looking for wedding or engagement rings. The moment you see a ring on that finger that looks like it could be prenuptial or the knot itself, check the finger on the right hand. Sometimes girls just like to wear rings on their ring fingers so they neutralize it by wearing one on both. If there is you could still be in with a chance. This should rapidly become instinctive, like looking in the mirror of a car. It will save you all sorts of time, embarrassment and physical damage.

Let's look at a sales assistant. If she seems single, and friendly, try and extend the transaction. Maintain eye contact, smile a lot, and try and prolong the meeting. Ask questions, check different products out, leave a tip. Keep

Sex tip no. 9: Sexual Diseases

There's so many of these now that's it's getting really frightening. This is no joke. The revolution is definitely over. Wife-swapping, swinging, orgies and the rest have been out of fashion for years: now they're positively out of bounds. Anyone can have something nasty so don't mess about with anyone whose family tree you can't trace back at least three generations. The simplest advice is proceed with caution and unless you're an Adonis-like heart-throb, think twice before leaping into bed with someone who seems to be throwing herself at you. Ask yourself why she is lavishing all this immediate attention on you. Why aren't there other men around? Do they know something you don't? Stay suspicious.

---

your friendliness within the bounds of friendly believability though. In shops it's always worth looking for something quite high up, then when the girl reaches it you can leap in and give her a hand. This is always an exceptionally good start.

As long as the girl is working somewhere you can return, don't take any very bold steps on this first meeting, like asking her name, or asking her out. Most daylighters cultivate first in a lot of places and reap later as they become available. Make a point of then going back the next day and buying something else. On this second meeting try swapping names. If this works, and she freely gives hers, this is a tenuous display of intent. Conclude the second meeting by asking for a veiled date (following shortly).

The thing about daylight is that it should never really stop. It isn't a substitute for nightlifing, it is a continuous low-risk accompaniment to it, almost like going for a forecast bet rather than a favourite to win. Whenever you're out and about you should be keeping your eyes open for girls, and any reasonable situation where you can gain some degree of familiarity should be seized. The nice thing about daylighting is that it normally lacks the terrible time pressure you get at night. You can come back at the end of the day without having found a girl. It's okay because that wasn't the main purpose of the day. It was only a subsidiary purpose. You had to go to work, or to shop anyway. This continuous nature of the technique should be observed in individual encounters. Try and build up a network of girls that you come across regularly. Get to know them, then when you feel the moment is right, ask them out.

One word of warning: beware of asking out girls when they work at shops or restaurants which you really enjoy going to, or couldn't do without. If they say no, or say yes and the date goes all wrong, it's very hard to go back to the shop or restaurant afterwards. It's best to save dates and familiarity for less important places.

The Veiled Date

The veiled date is basically a rhetorical question.

GUY: Hi there, Diane, how's the day been?
SALES GIRL: Oh, not so bad, the same old things.
GUY: Huh, yeah, know what you mean. Look have you got any dental floss?
GIRL: Sure, 25p.
GUY: Thanks. (*Pause.*) Listen, it would be really good to get together some time, go out and have a drink or something.

At this point the male acts very casually, grabbing his bag and looking very obviously on his way out so there is no question of him staying. But he is searching for every flicker of expression on the girl's face. If all has gone well she'll say.

SALES GIRL: That'd be really nice.

The man then leaves. He knows he's got an initial victory, and he can afford to break it up and enjoy it for a couple of days. A few days later he can actually propose the date.

With girls you meet on pure one-offs, girls who happen to sit opposite you on the tube, or queue next to you in the bank, you're in a much more difficult situation. Here nightlife tactics prevail. You know if you don't act you'll probably never see her again, but the action is high-risk because you generally have no indication of how interested she is in you. Try and get a dash of eye contact (although this is a nauseatingly inaccurate measurement of female interest), but accept the fact that you're probably going to have to decide if you're in a sufficiently ebullient mood to make a wild gesture without having any idea what the reaction will be. Although the ad is stupid, the principle behind the guy who spots a girl he thinks is fantastic when she walks past, buys her a bunch of flowers, and then rushes out after her, gives them to her, and ends up having a drink with her, is absolutely right. And often, the girl is so suprised and naturally flattered (though also a little embarrassed), that she will accept a date on the spot. Flowers are a little ostentatious, but small gifts, a sandwich, a postcard, a key ring – something a little bit off-beat and silly – make good opening gambits. Then you just go for the date. Generally keep the date to a lunchtime. Lunches are very neutral (although US motel owners point out that more four-hour rentings occur between the hours of one and five than any other time of the day). Evenings and weekends are for more intimate acquaintances and later dates. Although acceptance rates are high, so are no-shows. Something like 60 per cent of these dates don't happen because the girl gets cold feet, so don't let all satisfaction ride on the meeting. Enjoy the bravado of having got the date in the first place.

Asking a Girl Out

There are many different ways of asking someone out and many different things to do; however, there are two rules and trends which are worth observing and knowing about. The percentage date request is a daytime date. A girl really has to be very involved with someone else or not interested at all to say no to lunch. Dinners are loaded with all sorts of unanswered questions – Where's the coffee going to be drunk? Are there going to be any night-caps? Your car or hers? Does the man expect something in return? Many men now opt for sports dates which can be in the evening, but remain neutral because they lack the romantic associations of dinner. An invitation to go and play squash, to go swimming, to play tennis, to come jogging. All have high rates of success. Weekend dates are slightly curious. Weekends aren't as high risk as evenings, but they are considered more intimate than lunches. Steer away from Saturday nights, which are always booked up. Sunday mornings and Sunday lunchtimes can actually make quite good neutral times.

How to ask a girl out

The key is to make the date request as much unlike a premeditated request as possible. The more planned it appears, the more the girl will wonder what exactly you have in mind. If she senses that you have been plotting the whole thing out, she'll start looking for the small print in the contract. Try and make your request sound as much like a last-minute request as possible.

Let's look at the sales assistant again:

GUY: I know, it's amazing how busy it can get.
GIRL: Yeah, anyway, I suppose I'd better be going now.
GUY: Me too, I'm starving, I've got to go and get something to eat. (*Pause.*) Hey, you must be hungry too, why don't we go around the corner and grab a pizza?
GIRL: Okay, that'd be nice.

Cardinal errors include the blanket technique, which not only has a high failure rate but actually annoys girls beyond all measure.

GUY: Hey, listen, what are you doing on Thursday night?

The unwritten rule is that you give a girl a specific proposal, a time and an activity, but never just the time. This puts them on the spot. If they say, 'nothing' and let you continue they are having to say that they are actually quite interested in your company above and beyond anything that you might suggest the two of you doing. Girls don't like this. They like to keep you guessing, and overall it's best to keep them sweet. They always find a way of getting you back.

The second most cardinal of errors is the excessively negative date proposition. In the game of sexual pursuit, a bad attitude is self-fulfilling. It comes true.

GUY (*nervously, already depressed*): I don't suppose you'd have any interest in coming out for a pizza?
GIRL: No. No interest.

Another very good safety ploy is to wrap a date up so that it doesn't sound so one on one. This is like giving a dash of lunchtime neutrality to what is otherwise an unremittingly after hours, passionate evening rendezvous. So instead of saying, 'I was wondering if you'd be interested in coming to see *Cats*, and then going on to dinner?' you say, 'Look, a whole bunch of us are going along to *Cats* and then out to dinner and I was wondering whether you'd like to come along too?'

This increases your chances of acceptance by about 60 per cent (anything over one couple is a 'whole bunch'). The only drawback with these dates is that it makes you susceptible to the girl who is basically not that interested in you, but thinks she might meet some interesting people through you, or at least get some nice theatre visits.

Coping With a No

Watch carefully how a girl says no. The nature of the male is such, so crushingly sensitive, so appallingly insecure, that any reason the girl gives for not being able to come will immediately be rejected as complete fabrication.

GUY: I was wondering if you'd like to pop out for something to eat?
GIRL: Oh, thanks, that's really nice of you but I've got to go and meet my aunt.
GUY: Oh, well, maybe another time.
EGO (*over*): Lying bitch, she saw the spot on your neck. Why does she think she's so good, she's not even that good-looking. Oh god I'm depressed, why did she have to say no, why doesn't she like me . . . etc.

In fact, though, if she seems to have made a plausible excuse, especially if it's right off the top of her head, give her the benefit of the doubt. Once. Leave it a week or so and then ask her again. If you get another excuse your ego was right and you need to run for it.

Notes

Basically note-droppers are wimps. Writing a date request down, handing it to the target, and then running for it is a coward's ploy. It screams bad acne as a teenager, it screams, 'I don't expect you to say yes.' Yet astonishingly it is a very effective method. Girls don't seem to pick up the wimpish vibes or if they do, find them attractive. The note success rate is very high, but you need to give your note a little twist to make it really effective. Let's look at the nightclub note. It already has some momentum on its side the moment it's delivered because the chances are that the receiver won't have got any others that night. So it's going to have her attention. Now given that she's amused and paying attention and you haven't got to perform in public, you can afford to try and hot dog it a little. You can't be too imperative:

MEET ME AT THE CIGARETTE MACHINE AT 10.30 P.M.

is wrong. This makes her feel like a sex thrall, a slave to your overpowering attractiveness, if she turns up. You have to be more sensitive, amuse her, make it easy for her to accept.

I HEAR THERE'S AN EXCEPTIONALLY GOOD CABARET AT 10.30 OUT BY THE CIGARETTE MACHINE. I WOULD BE HONOURED IF YOU WOULD JOIN ME IN MY BOX

(This is an actual note which did work.)

A little bit of humour, a little bit of manners, a basic statement of intent. When you hand over the note, pause for a moment so that she can get a good look at you, and then retreat.

Choose the meeting place carefully. You want it to be somewhere relatively quiet, and also a little out in the open with one or two alcoves nearby, or a lavatory. You can then hang out by the alcove, or the area near the lavatory and watch the chosen place until her arrival. Don't wait right in the centre of the rendezvous spot. This leaves you open to persecution by male friends of the target. Stay hidden until she comes, check she's alone, and then move out to greet her, making out you were a little held up because you bumped into someone you used to know. You can then proceed as normal, bearing in mind that you're already fairly advanced. Such a note acceptance is equivalent to a slow dance acceptance.

If she doesn't show up at the meeting place on time, give her fifteen minutes. If she still hasn't come, give up and make a point of avoiding the part of the club she was in for the rest of the evening.

Notes are equally effective in daylight situations.

The wimp request

There is one exception to all the date request rules just given. The girl who is attracted to nervous, insecure men. The slightest tremble, the faintest quaver in the voice, the tiniest bead of sweat on the forehead, to this type of girl these are powerful aphrodisiacs. In fact in one American survey it was found that the most effective form of introduction from a man to a woman that he's never met before is, 'This sounds, stupid, and I'm feeling very awkward, but would you like to dance?' The thing about wimps is that they are being honest, and it adds a humanizing touch to the proceedings. Marilyn Monroe-types used to the slick, fast car, Wham! suburban types are, according to legend, tremendously attracted to this nervousness, so don't despair if you feel all this planning and concern for details isn't for you.

The only problem is that these girls are very difficult to identify. Ironically enough it's often the most macho sort of girl who's most attracted to the wimpish sort of man. The sort of girl who wears black leather, chained belts, very dark eye make-up, pointed winklepicker boots with stiletto heels, chain smokes and glowers rather than smiles. The more nervous the man gets, the more aroused the girl becomes.

The problem is that given a choice more girls will go for the Mel Gibson type than the Woody Allen type, which means that the chronically nervous, even though they will get some yesses, will probably get a lot more nos.

Telephones

Telephones are terribly hard machines to use effectively. They seem to make the best jokes sound corny, the toughest men feel wimps, the most delightful dates sound dreary. Yet a fancied girl's phone number remains one of the most treasured possessions known to man. Cold calls are hardest, calls where you've found a girl's number yourself, through her friends or through work, a call which she won't be expecting at all, and yet one which is proposing a date which you both know is designed to end in a pass. Cold calls should decrease in frequency as you get older, but they never lose their ability to terrify.

Using the telephone

The first thing to remember is that you're calling a girl to offer something nice, a meal, a movie, something essentially pleasant which you're saying you're willing to pay for. You're not a tabloid journalist ringing up to offer her money in return for spilling the dirt on her mother's relationship with a 'Crossroads' star. Secondly, the worst thing she can say is no. For some reason a no on the phone is worse than a no in a nightclub, even though it's far more private. This is probably for the same reason that a mistake in golf is far worse than a mistake in tennis – you've got so much more time to think about it, to turn it over in your mind, to agonize over it. In tennis matches and nightclubs you're thrown right back into the thick of things. In golf and on the phone you're left alone to worry about it. So whenever you're making a major date phone call make it just before a period of frantic activity like shopping, laundry or squash.

Second, you've got to try and make the date and your voice sound as casual as possible. A good way of doing this, and of giving the call a novel disguise which could well amuse the girl too, is to make it from a coinbox actually during another activity. For instance, if you're out shopping, do it between stores, if you're at the sports club, do it between matches. The pips, the money, the lack of time, the surprise, all give a general impression of spontaneity. This is important in a cold call because if she stops to think about it she'll know that you've plotted to get hold of her phone number. This method keeps you looking cool.

Coinbox calls also have the added bonus of restricting the time you can speak, as well as supplying a perfect pause, in the initial pips, for you to hang up without losing face, in the event of her father or elder brother picking up the phone, or if you just lose your nerve. The good thing about keeping the phone call short is that it prevents your nerves from taking control. Without the pips after two minutes your weaker side will spin out some ridiculous conversation about appallingly trivial topics in the hope of putting off the evil moment when the date request has to be made.

A bad phone call

CALLER: Hello, could I speak to Jane.
JANE: Speaking.
CALLER: Hi, oh, hi, it's Greg here, bit of a surprise, huh, met you at Simon's last Sunday.
JANE: Oh, yes.
CALLER: Anyway, I was amazed by the weather on Sunday, weren't you? I mean it was so changeable.
JANE: Yes, I suppose so.
CALLER: All that sun, then all that rain. Still the food was really good. Talking about food I had a great meal last night in this new Indian . . . etc.

so the conversation will continue until

CALLER: . . . with these two footballers on either side getting into their car. It was so funny, I wish you could have seen it and would you like to come to the cinema next Wednesday evening?

By this time, the girl is probably so bored and so aware of your stalling tactics that she can't wait for you to ask so that she can say no and get off the phone. Often, if the nerves get on top at the start, the caller will wimp out of asking altogether and will end up just saying goodbye after a ridiculous conversation with a complete stranger. This burns any chance of future success with the girl. The fact is it gets harder to ask the girl out the longer you wait. Ask first, chat later.

Lots of the mistakes tend to crop up too when a nervous male has too much time on the phone. On a cold call you should never start apologetically explaining how you got the girl's number. It doesn't make any difference how you got it. If she likes you she won't mind. If she doesn't, she'll say no anyway and you'll never see her again. It just makes you feel nervous, and sound apologetic, and this starts making the girl think that maybe she should be pissed off because you've taken liberties.

Also try to keep the call up-beat and to the point.

A good phone call

Based on an original transcript from a successful phone date.

Pips go
MALE CALLER (*pretending*): Oh hang on, the coin's jammed, woah, okay, it's in. Hello?
GIRL: Hello?
MALE: Hi, Jane, it's me, Paul, I met you last week at Simon's. Look, sorry about all the confusion but I think this coinbox is pre-war.
GIRL: Oh, that's okay.
MALE: Anyway, look, I've got to dash, there's a whole bunch of people waiting for me and I've got no more 10ps. I was just wondering if you'd like to come and play tennis next weekend? There's a whole load of us going down to the club. It should be really good fun.
JANE: Oh, well, when exactly?
MALE: Twelve o'clock, Saturday. I'll come by and pick you up.
JANE: Er, okay, that'd be fun.
MALE: Right. Bye. See you then.

There are so many bits of this call that are right that it's difficult to know where to begin. It's spontaneous, he lets Jane know that he's with friends and in a hurry, putting him in a position of strength, he makes it a general date, plus a weekend one, thereby building up his percentage of success. It's got a bit of humour, it's relaxed, it's polite. How could she say no? It was, of course, all bullshit, but it sounded great.

CHAPTER 4

The Night of the Date

There are two broad schools of thought when it comes to preparing for dates. One says always give yourself enough time to get home before the date so that you can gather your resources and put the finishing touches to your appearance. A day in the office obviously leaves you a little worn and torn, showers and fresh clothes can make a difference. But the other school, which prefers the date commencing right after work, says that that hour of preparation gives far too much time for thought and nerves. Dates, like date requests, tend to work better when they're as spontaneous as possible.

What's the answer?

A balance is probably the best thing. Leave time for a change of clothes before the date but whatever happens don't wash your hair before going out. Freshly washed hair can start drying so strangely, the strangeness being directly proportionate to the importance of the date. Wash hair the day before so it still looks fresh but is definitely under control. During the day of the date itself pursue a hands-off policy. Consult only friendly mirrors, and in the event of any blemishes being sighted, lay off them. Don't at all costs embark on any major cosmetic surgery, particularly involving spots.

Bad date preparation

8.15 a.m. Rise and go straight to the bathroom to check face for obvious, recently arrived blemishes. Eyes moderately bloodshot. Medium-sized bags under eyes which should clear up by mid-morning. The slight reddish patch just beside my nose on the left has erupted in the night into an asymmetrical patch of acne. No sign of a head yet.

10.30 a.m. Third trip to the lavatory this morning to check on the progress of the spot.

11.00 a.m. Tried lancing the spot to force a head and it is now growing faster than before. Black bags not clearing up.

12.30 p.m. Ate a cheese and onion sandwich before realizing what I'd done. Definite smell of onion on my breath. One bag has cleared up. Spot holding firm.

3.30 p.m. Got that itchy scalp feeling twenty minutes ago. Held off for fifteen minutes then had to give it a good scratch. Dandruff everywhere. Onion smell still lingering despite the afternoon of chewing gum. Second bag still hasn't gone. Spot is growing again.

7.00 p.m. She's due in twenty minutes. I'm now washing my hair again because it dried all strangely the first time round. It's the Head and Shoulders, I'm not used to the thickness of the shampoo.

The onion taste persists despite the gobs of toothpaste I've been chewing. The spot and one bag remain. I can feel my tummy slightly overhanging the waistband of my trousers.

I wish I hadn't eaten that Danish for breakfast and had found time to take some exercise yesterday.

11.30 p.m. Watching the late movie, picking my spot, scratching my scalp. She didn't show up.

Dinner Dates

If it's a dinner date there are some important rules which need to be observed. All of these apply to the choice of food.

First, it's completely off to start worrying about the price

Sex tip no. 10: Hair Gel

Hair gel is a fantastic invention, opening up to the hopeful suburban playboy styling opportunities previously reserved for girls and salons. It hides dandruff, it hides greasy hair, it makes anyone look clean by giving them a freshly showered look. However, you should use it carefully. Don't go for a radical hair shape on a big date. The problem with hair gel is that although it makes your hair look wet, it in fact dries rock hard. Now with something as visible as a full head of apparently soaking wet hair, you need to have an answer to any inquiries about why it's taking so long to dry. If it's going to be a relatively short meeting you can go in with a 'I've just played a squash match and showered' line (which is great). However, if you're going out on a lengthy date you're taking a big risk with this line because you're inviting exposure. She's bound to notice that it stays wet and then you're going to have to admit that you lied. Quite apart from anything else, if the date goes well the girl will probably want to touch your hair at some point. Then you're really up shit creek. So this means that you have to come clean the moment she asks the first question. Say that you can't stand it when your fringe hangs in your eyes and that your hair has got so long that it's the best way to keep it back. Not sounding like you're making an excuse, just casual and conversational. Basically try and laugh it off.

In fact when it comes to laughing it off the great thing about modern hair gel over ancient Brylcreem is that it has a built-in safety mechanism for those moments when you've talked yourself into a terrible corner. Let's say you've gone in hard with a 'I've just showered' line, and she's bought it for about twenty minutes. But then quite suddenly, she leans over and somehow touches your hair. She recoils in shock. You try and talk your way out of it, relying on the 'it keeps my fringe out of my eyes', or 'I didn't get a chance to wash it' line. But she isn't smiling, or understanding. She's feeling cheated, and looking at you oddly. You have to act fast. You can't sit there the rest of the evening with a mop of contentious gelled hair. The safety mechanism, one of the great wonders of modern hairdressing science, is right at your fingertips. Literally.

All you have to do is run your hands through the gel twice, and the wet look miraculously vanishes, leaving in its place a sort of swept back, rather neat, Fergel Sharkey sort of coiffure. It may feel like a major swallowing of pride to do it, but you've got to give the rest of the date a chance of succeeding. Leave the bone of contention there, and you're shot down in flames before you've even taken off.

---

of the meal – if you're having to make your choice from the menu after your date's selection on the basis of what you can afford you're in deep trouble. Poverty, like meanness, is never an attractive trait. Choose a restaurant where you know you can afford to eat properly, and if in doubt scale down and eat up rather than eating up and having to scale down with the menu. You want to look flamboyant and relaxed, not penny-pinching and up-tight. No, the key to your menu selection should be based, like an athlete's, on generating peak performance in what will hopefully follow. The problem with certain combinations of very rich food, especially if swilled down with wine, is that mixed with a slightly nervous stomach they can produce wind. And there is nothing more destructive to passion and romance than wind. Burping is bad, farting is final.

Many men over-confidently plough on through the rich sauces, and heavy wines, and won't even go to the lavatory before leaving. Then, after seating the woman in the car and shutting the door, they fart as they walk around to the driver's door. This seems a fairly safe way of getting rid of the wind, except that wind tends to cling to your clothing. If you fart and then get straight into the car, a large part of the fart comes in with you. Needless to say this is extremely embarrassing. Having to walk around the car three times before getting in is also rather hard to explain away. So if you're going to be cavalier about your food, give yourself plenty of private open-air time to dissipate it.

It's much easier to eat lighter, plainer food during the meal, avoiding orange juice and sparkling mineral water which brews wind like yoghurt and muesli.

Nightclubs: Asking a Girl to Dance

All the preparations are complete, clothes, hair, anti-perspirant, gob of toothpaste on the tongue, pack of Durex in your pocket in case you get lucky. You've arrived at the club or disco and you're ready to find a girl. First, some simple rules.

Never go out to clubs with groups of single men if you're hoping to try and find girls. These mass outings are simply too pressurized. If seven guys all arrive at the same nightclub at the same time you will all feel a desperate pressure to succeed in front of your mates, or at least not be seen to have failed. You're always trying to

---

Sex tip no. 11: Group Sex

The great wife-swapping and orgy days are over now, only the scraps are left among the more depressing suburban types. This is definitely a good thing, because for the standard British temperament, group sex is not a satisfying experience. It's rather like having a Chinese meal. Everyone orders a different course, and then you all just grab at the same time. The result is intense frustration as other people seem to be monopolizing the best dishes. To be avoided.

---

be talking to someone, and not get left on the edge of a group chatting up some women, looking stupid and ignored. All the pressures that anyone would normally feel are heightened a thousand times.

If you go out with one other guy, spend some time together having the traditional nervous conversation at the bar, but when it's time to start looking, split up and arrange to meet somewhere a little later. Otherwise the same pressures apply, you have to look for girls in pairs, one of you always gets no girl, or the ugly girl, awkward threesomes crop up. The whole thing is a disaster. And when you're sitting at the bar having your awkward conversation with him beforehand try and avoid slipping into the standard topic of 'how ridiculous these nightclub places are for picking up girls'. This is always an excuse, a way of making it okay if you fail. You've got to learn to enjoy competing, and not worry too much about winning or losing so that all you can do is bitch about the club or the music or your luck while you wait for some wonderful woman to fall unasked into your lap.

Example of a bad conversation

Two guys sitting in a nightclub, surrounded by music, by women, eating too many hula hoops, grinning with gritted bonhomie, laughing too loudly at each other's jokes.

GUY: I mean, I don't know about you but I hate these places, I mean it's so crazy. I could stay here all night just looking at the ridiculous way people try and pick each other up.

GUY 2: Oh, yeah, absolutely, it's all so artificial, especially here. The music's too loud to have a real conversation, the girls just aren't really that good-looking, and the dance floor is way too small.

During the conversation, which goes on in this vein for about four hours until they pluck up enough courage to go hunting solo, they are perpetually gazing longingly at

Sex tip no. 12: 'Value for Money'

There is a growing practice among the younger generation of heterosexual men to classify dates in terms of what you can roughly expect in return, and then to subtract from, or multiply your preferred type of date depending on how much you want or can afford. Some use the system well, generally those who are always dating girls from the same demographic and teenage party background. Everyone knows what is supposed to equal what. Spread your net a little wider and trouble starts.

Anyway the basis of the system is this: one major meal at a fairly good restaurant (with wine, candles, and at least two knives in each place setting, say £15 a head plus) equals heavy petting. Two dinners of this calibre, with a spattering of phone calls thrown in in between, equals one screw. The mathematicians among the ranks of the romantically underprivileged rationalize this still further by saying if one screw equals approximately £40, then nine dinners at Macdonalds, ten trips to the cinema, three to the theatre, or thirty-eight to Madame Tussaud's equal the same thing. It may seem crude to work it out quite so coldly based on the financial cost of each date, but in fact it does have a logic of its own.

Cheaper dates require frequent repetition over a longer period of time, by the end of which, unless something has gone terribly wrong, everything should be heading that way anyway. Expensive evening dates automatically have all sorts of romantic overtones which act as a great inflamer of passion and therefore reduce the time required before the big bang.

---

girls walking in and out, and trying to talk themselves into a frame of mind in which they'll be able to ask one of them to dance.

How to detect a bad attitude

If you find yourself leaning on a bar in an appropriately secluded corner, watching what's going on, you'll notice a tendency to focus on certain girls, and to keep drawing your gaze back to them. You start hoping that they will turn your way and then return your gaze (although the moment they do you turn away immediately). You wonder what it would be like to press their heads into your chest, and run your tongue along their teeth.

This means you fancy them.

As you watch them, probably standing with a small group of friends, various single men will approach the group and try and latch onto certain members and then neatly manoeuvre them away. The girls will usually resist these attempts until Mr Right (for the night) crops up. The man with a Bad Attitude will watch the various male aggressors approach with an air somewhere between contempt and acidic sneering. He will search the male for signs of nervousness, awkwardness, he will mercilessly grade his physical appearance, his clothes sense, whether he smokes, how he drinks, searching relentlessly for defects more completely than even the choosiest of girls. As the male messes up, is rejected, and gradually squeezed out, the Bad Attitude will hungrily clutch every ego-shattering detail of his failure, stretching each one out, savouring every exquisite moment of it. Not because of jealousy, but because IT CONFIRMS HIS OWN WORST FEARS OF HOW AWFUL IT WILL BE WHEN HE TOO IS REJECTED. This isn't sadism. This is sado-masochism. And it's all wrong. Don't look for proofs of why it won't do any good to go and ask someone to dance. Don't enjoy other males' failures. Learn from them. Watch their mistakes. Remember them. And don't repeat them. The object here is to get out of your corner into their corner. Not to stay in your corner, chuckling in a resigned, worldly-wide manner.

Things not to do

Don't start opening a packet of cigarettes the moment you start talking to the girl, and then go through and nervously light the one you take out, and pull long and hard, sucking in breaths as if you've just been winded and are gasping for air. This gives away the fact that you are nervous. Don't start gulping down the junk food left on the counter. Don't look desperately round the club when you can't think of anything to say. Don't play air guitar when you can't think of anything to say. Don't finger any spots you may be worrying about. Don't look directly at her breasts. Don't touch your erection.

The Club Routine

Okay, you're by yourself, you're into the nightclub, and you're ready for action. What do you do? The first thing is to find where the lavatories are and check that it's a good mirror. On the way in you should have looked for neutral sitting areas, places away from the main action where you can come to recuperate, nurse any wounds, and pluck up courage for another sortie. These are often near the lavatory. The lavatory is the central HQ for the evening. You will be coming and going throughout the night so get acquainted with it, and if the mirror inside isn't a good one, don't use it. Otherwise you'll never ask anyone. You should have used your good mirror last thing before leaving home, so the one at the nightclub is just a checker. Generally though they're good, being lit along the rim, or from above in the centre of the room, in strips. This leaves you slightly in the shade, making you look a little tanned, and the synthetic light is normally quite soft, hiding spots and highlighting features.

Okay, the first step is to find a good place to sit. Most people go to the bar, and this has its advantages, mainly that you are absorbed into a general area of activity so that even when no one is talking to you you don't look left out.

But they're sometimes quite difficult places to watch the rest of the club from, and also many girls have already been apprehended by the time they've got there.

A better place is somewhere slightly raised, not too far from the bar, where you can lean and watch without being too visible. The first thing is just to practise standing by yourself, watching. Don't think about asking anyone for a dance, don't think about whether any girls are looking at you. Just watch, listen to the music, and let your nerves subside. Gradually the tension and the initial feeling of awkwardness that usually walks into nightclubs with the single male, fades. You'll hear a couple of tunes you like, you'll see a couple of funny things, you'll actually start enjoying yourself, even though you're by yourself. If you've never felt like this, go out soon, by yourself, and practise.

Once you've got this under control you need to get your look right. Don't sneer. Don't look nervous. Just try and smile with a sort of newborn innocent smile, the smile of a sensitive (though still a tough man) who has just returned from twelve years in the jungle, or twelve years in jail, and is just pleased to be here, in the club, around people having fun. After a bit, it will become more natural and you'll notice that people don't all start pointing at you, moving away slightly, or laughing under their breath.

FACT: it is the overriding impression of many single men entering nightclubs that many other co-clubbers notice every stupid thing they do, are watching them to see if they know anyone, are searching their clothes for a mark of bad taste. The pressure of this scrutiny is immense. However, the fact of the matter is that nobody else really cares. They're too busy worrying about their own spots, their own dance technique, their own female targets. You're operating alone. Relax.

Once you've got used to this look, and this feeling of gentle, unobserved singleness, the desperate drive to always pretend that although it looks like you're not with someone else, in fact you actually are, melts away.

You can afford to stay in one place for up to thirty

minutes before moving on. More than thirty minutes and people will begin to think that you aren't able to find anyone to dance with, or else that you've been stood up. So spend the first thirty minutes getting into the mood (if you need that long) and then go for a walk around the club.

Now the rules for walking are slightly different. Don't walk around enjoying everything too much, this is considered unattractive and distasteful. When you're on the move take advantage of your appearance of purpose. Walk with a determined step, looking quite intensely ahead, as if for someone you've arranged to meet. Then get back to the lavatory, take a breather, come back in, find a new place, and focus on a girl.

The getting of the girl

Find a girl who is in the right division for you, unless you're feeling confident in which case you can go ahead and play up a division. Ideally she will be with a group of other girls. Not too small, or else she'll be reluctant to leave them, not by herself, because then she'll probably be with someone else. Watch her for a bit, check she is unaccompanied, and then prepare to ask her to dance.

At this stage you will suddenly find a million reasons for not asking, why you haven't got time, or don't really like her. You'll suddenly remember you had to call that friend of yours, or that you'll look a lot more relaxed with a drink, or that you'll just go to the lavatory then the moment you get back you'll do it. Your breath will also get short, your heart will be beating so hard you can't help but feel it's visible. All in all you're on the verge of the classic, mammoth wimp-out. Men have felt like this ever since they first asked women to dance.

You *must* confront it, and deal with it. Going to a night-club always offers you two choices – ask and maybe get turned down, or don't ask and never know. Which of the two feels worse when you're going home at the end of the evening?

No comfort here, I'm afraid. There's no doubt that getting turned down is the worst thing that can happen. Not daring to ask at least leaves you with dreams, you can fantasize. Asking, and being refused, is so complete, so black, and so depressing that nothing else comes close. However, taking that risk is the price of having a yes which is so nice, so inspiring, and so much fun that it'll keep you coming back and trying for years.

Just this night, ask. The chances are that eventually someone will say yes.

So what do you do?

You take a deep breath, walk up to the girl, look at her, forget that all her friends turn round too, and say, 'Would you like to dance?'

Five words, maybe a five-foot walk. It can be done. Providing you consider this first run as a warm-up, a way of loosening your arm, of trying out your technique, and not worrying too much about whether the ball goes in or out, it's okay. The key is getting the words out to a live girl. That breaks the spell.

And providing you've picked her properly the chances are she'll say yes. Girls go to nightclubs to be asked to dance by males even though the males manage to persuade themselves that they go simply to sneer at and embarrass the lines of poor, unfortunate men who throw their egos at their feet.

A typical conversation that an embarrassed man thinks he will have with a girl of his choice when he asks her to dance:

MALE (*breathless with nerves*): Excuse me, I was just wondering whether you might like to dance?

The girl turns, all her friends turn too, as do two other rather large men talking to the group. They all sneer at the same time.

ONE OF THE MEN: Cyndi? Is this guy bothering you? Would you like me to remove him?

CYNDI (the girl of his choice): He asked me to dance. He has a spot on his nose, there is some dandruff on his collar and he asked me to dance. (*The other girls look aghast.*)
OTHER MAN: The sick bastard. You pervert.
(*Other people look round, the male blushes so hard sweat bursts through the layers of Amplex under his arm.*)
OTHER MAN: Get back to your bathroom and masturbate like you did last night.

It may sound ridiculous read in the light of day, but somehow, on the verge of action, such scenes become incredibly possible, even probable.

Don't ask her if she wants a drink. Don't just start a conversation. Get right to the point. Simply ask her to dance. This gives her a clear choice to make.

If she says yes it doesn't mean you've won, but it does mean you've taken a positive first step. She is returning the ball. She is considering the situation. Everything is still possible. Move straight to the dance floor, and if all you can think of to say is, 'God, the music's loud I can hardly hear myself speak', don't say anything.

If she says 'no', get out fast. Don't be tempted to linger, or say, 'oh, come on, just this once'. Certainly don't start asking all the other girls in the group (they are hardly going to take goods that have been publicly rejected no matter whether they're interested or not). By turning down an invitation to dance the girl is saying she is not interested. Don't stay in her area but move into a new patch with entirely fresh talent.

Coping with the no

It's going to sting, but you'll notice if you go back to your original smile, and 'it's okay to be by myself' feeling, that it gradually melts away. In one evening it's emotionally possible to have anything up to five rejections, you just need to toughen out the first moments of nausea and suicidal depression and then try again. As long as you stay in the game your average will be okay, but you have to keep trying.

It may come as some small consolation to know that even the best-looking men in history have been frequently rejected, and that a girl can have a thousand reasons for rejecting you entirely unrelated to your looks. You may look like her old boyfriend, she may be allergic to blonds, you may be too good looking for her. Clutch at these straws, believe in them, do whatever you have to do to stay in the running. If you get turned down more than five times in the same evening your luck is seriously out or your technique is seriously flawed. In both cases give up for the night and go back to page 1. Underestimate yourself this time, play down one division, and go slowly.

On the Dance Floor

Starting with a fast dance is pretty easy. The floor is almost always too crowded for anyone to see what you're doing too clearly and the trend in contemporary nightclubbing is for erratic, slightly awkward movements anyway. Unless you're really bad you'll get by.

If you are really bad, and feel really awkward out there, the key is to move your forearms up and down, from the elbows, in time with the music. Many dancers leave their arms out of things completely, concentrating everything on their legs and feet, actually leaning over and staring at them. But if what your feet are doing is weak you won't want to draw attention to them, so keep your head up, stick your hands out in front of you, palms up, and move them up and down in time with the music. Don't click your fingers. This is an excellent start to almost any dance.

One of the perennial problems of dancing with a stranger is that it's difficult to look at them face to face without feeling stupid or embarrassed. Vacantly staring over their shoulder into the middle distance is, however, not much better. Cultivate a slightly more upbeat version of the 'I'm really enjoying this as a night out quite apart from any success I may or may not have with women' smile, look at other dancers, and lean forward occasionally to point something out to your partner. The volume of the music normally makes physical contact almost inevitable here, you have to lean forward and shout into her ear. Watch very carefully how she responds to this physical contact. If she seems to warm to it, especially if she leans forward and shouts back to you *with her hand on your shoulder*, you know you're doing well.

Try and keep her on the dance floor for a second fast dance. If she wants to get back to her friends you could be in trouble, left standing on the fringes of their conversation feeling out of place. Try to buy her a drink and keep the conversation going, but if she seems to tire of it and starts looking around at other males, get out fast. Nothing is more pitiful than the sight of men standing beside bored girls, hands in pockets, nodding vacantly, nervously smiling, desperately drawing out the relationship in the hope of some heaven-sent change of fortune.

If she agrees to stay for a second fast dance you are moving on very well. This is universally accepted as a gesture of positive interest, and now you can try increasing the degree and frequency of the physical contact. Occasionally put your hands on her shoulders (in a playful, unthreatening manner) during some songs, and if things are really going well, on her hips. You can relax more, even swing her round a bit. At the end of this dance it's time to pause for a serious drink and chat.

If possible keep her away from her original group of friends. Take her with you to the bar, and fight for service together. Start talking about who she is, what her line of work is etc. while you're waiting for the slow music to start.

Don't succumb to the temptation to drain your drink and suggest a dance the moment that the slow music starts (known as 'grope music' in the trade). You have to be carefully watching for signals at every stage. Wait for the floor to fill with couples, make sure there is some passionate activity going on, and then engineer a pause in the conversation and gaze towards the floor. Her eyes will inevitably follow yours. Watch the groping and the hugging and the sighing for a moment, just long enough to establish beyond all doubt that she has understood the full implications of a slow dance, and then turn back and continue the conversation neutrally for another couple of minutes. Only then should you ask her to dance.

If she says yes

SLOW DANCE SEQUENCE (see page 77).

If she says no, get out fast and begin again.

Parties

Parties, even the very largest parties, are much more difficult situations to meet girls than nightclubs, or any daylight venues. Whereas in a nightclub, or a shop, it's quite easy to be alone, to be waiting to act, or buy something, at a party, a guest by himself for more than about two minutes becomes a social leper. Everyone needs to be seen to be convivial, to be known. Attractiveness in a party atmosphere means, above all else, being part of the set, a person with friends, relaxed, comfortable, at ease. If you look isolated and ignored, no other guest will dare talk to you for fear of being tarred with the same brush.

So what's your primary goal?

First it's to find someone to talk to. Fast.

You've got roughly five minutes. During that time you can hang up your coat, get a drink, and look briefly around. For those five minutes you can be alone, and seem to have a believable purpose.

Then you must find a conversation.

If you really don't know anyone the best thing to do is to find someone else who's looking isolated. Lepers tend

Sex tip: no. 13: Slow Dance Technique

If you've been at a party or disco and have asked a girl, whether you know her or not, if she'd like to dance to a fast tune, this gives you no claim on her affections. If however it is an obviously slow song, other couples are dancing slowly together, and the lights are dimmed, you know that she is relatively interested if she says yes. Start slowly with the 'Eastern' grip, place your hands on her hips and allow her to put hers round your neck. This is the natural 'shake hands' grip, the introductory stage. Wait for the dance to progress before deciding whether to make a pass. If she moves in closer so that your bodies are grazing this is a sign that her speculative interest is now confirmed. Don't panic or go too fast, remember that the key to a good pass is leaving yourself as many disguised escape routes as possible. Slide your hands into the 'Continental' grip, moving them round to the small of her back and then let them rest there, joined together. Don't, whatever happens, slip them down to her bottom at this stage. This is unutterably outré. You must observe the general code, don't go to base 2 too fast.

Stay relaxed. Wait and see if she snuggles in, try a little pressure on her lower back if she does. Her head should by now be fitted neatly and naturally into your chest and neck. Don't nuzzle, just increase the pressure with your head slightly. By now you will probably be getting an erection. This is natural and to be expected. If you've followed dress guidelines, your trousers won't be too tight so it won't need rapid readjustment. DON'T, whatever happens, start rubbing your erection on her leg. Don't let her feel the erection at any cost. This is pushing things ahead too fast. She might get frightened or start laughing. It is distinctly uncool because it's giving away that you really fancy her and yet she hasn't had to give anything away about her feelings for you. It's easy to avoid your partner feeling the erection by slightly altering your stance.

Stand less face on, move slightly off to the side so that your legs and hips are no longer facing each other straight on but are interlocked – her leg, your leg, her leg, your leg. Depending on which side your erection tends to hang or jut your stance will leave it bulging out past her hip and groin. This isn't an obvious manoeuvre, actually feels very comfortable, and is quite natural.

Before the end of the dance you have to make a decision. Do you pass now or later? Much of this is decided by your intuition. The odds are simple. If you still aren't sure of the degree of her interest you can take a chance and wait till the next dance. This is usually okay providing the DJ fades the next slow dance in fairly fast. Otherwise you can be left with a long awkward pause just standing on the floor facing one another. If you don't fill the pause effectively she'll start to move back to her seat at the side and then all the momentum is lost. Generally though if you've been talking to her for a while, then been for a couple of fast dances, then sat down again, then asked for a slow dance after you've both sat and watched other couples positively enclasped, you're respectably on for first base. How?

Slow dance technique is simple. Squeeze her a little, hug her a little, keep your erection well away from her legs, then just hold your head a little closer to hers. If you seem to be getting all the right signals or at least no wrong ones) you now have to make her raise her head giving you a shot at her lips. The technique is simple. Very suddenly raise your head as if looking over hers. She will immediately raise hers, to be left staring straight into your eyes. Now you land the kiss.

---

to congregate around bookshelves, drinks tables, and bowls of food, each location providing a sort of meagre cover to being alone. There's no problem striking up conversation; they'll leap at anything you say.

Sex tip no. 14: Nerves: Who Gets Them Most?

There is a long and boring debate still going on about who gets more nervous on dates, the men or the women. Many women contend that they do. They say that having to sit and wait for the man to do something is absolutely terrifying. They have no control over what might or might not be coming. It's an 'eternal queue for the dentist's chair' type of feeling. This is bad. The men on the other hand have to try and decide when is the right moment to try something, what the likelihood of the girl accepting is, and what exactly to do.

Whose role is harder?

The men's. Unquestionably. If he gets turned down, it's going to be after he's acted, and this hurts terribly. There's no room for excuses. He can't lie to himself. He made his intentions clear, and the girl said no. If the girl fails to have a pass made at her, it can hurt, but because she tried nothing there's still room for excuses to herself. She can make it all right in her head. Men have the worst job and are usually more nervous.

Nevertheless, girls are a little nervous too, and this needs to be taken into account. If a man is really dead-smooth (hair gel, calm voice, fast hands) she can sometimes lose her nerve. He's too confident, too collected, too much. So she pulls back.

If the man casually shows he's a little nervous too, it humanizes him, the girl feels she's not alone with the butterflies and a love machine, and there's an immediate affinity. Kisses are likely to break out all over.

Dug in with your conversational cover you can now look around the room at the girls.

Your next move depends on the type of party you're at. If it's a big dancing and getting off with people party then you can just follow nightclub rules. Find a girl, ask her to dance etc. If on the other hand it's a small, drinks and gossip party, your aim is to get a name and a phone number.

Find the girl you're really most interested in and watch the group she's in carefully. You should be looking for all the normal things. Is she single? Does she look friendly? Is she in your league? The moment she breaks away, to go for another drink, or join the queue for the lavatory, you then intercept her.

What do you say?

The key here is to avoid any sort of pick-up line. Pick-up lines have really faded right out of fashion. What you're after is something light and conversational. Steer clear of anything along the lines of 'It must be fate that emptied our glasses at the same time.'

Drinks party conversation can start from the simplest of remarks. The strength of the punch, the décor of the flat, the look of the other guests. Avoid the archetypal drinks party line asking how she knows the host. This is a good establishing shot a few questions into the conversation, but not as a starter. You need to amuse her first. Something relaxed and humorous, not too harsh. 'Is that a sanitary towel you're wearing or are you just a transvestite?' is a little too hard. 'I'm completely lost but you seem to know where you're going. Do you mind if I follow you?' is probably going to get you in further to start off with.

All you need then is a burst of conversation, the establishment of some basic shared interest (video nasties, zoos, Dutch seventeenth-century watercolours) and you can suggest a meeting to indulge your interest together.

CHAPTER 5

Making a Pass

The pass is what everything we've discussed so far has been leading up to. The derivation of the term has been lost in the sands of time and the gropings of history, but a form of it has existed in every major civilization known to man.

Every modern language has a word for it. It is a concept so rich with promise, so wired with booby traps that the linguistics have overlaid it with centuries of fascinating vocabulary. It is to sex what Clapham Junction is to Southern Region – the Great Gateway. Beyond the pass lies the promise your erection has been telling you about since your testicles dropped. The key to making an effective pass is to understand that your aim is not solely to lay your hands on parts of your partner's body which in the normal course of events are considered out of bounds. And to lay on those hands with a premeditated intent to undress, fondle, and generally escalate proceedings as far as physically possible given the prevailing limitations of space, time, and the girl in question.

No. The nature of an effective pass is twofold.

First, it is to engage the girl physically.

But second it is to provide you with as many effective escape routes as possible along the way so that if she decides to pull back suddenly, you can bale out with your honour still intact right up to the last moment.

Making it with a girl or not making it is not the point. It's all about not losing face. This doesn't mean that you have to go into sexual encounters with a defensive attitude. It does mean that you go in with an alert attitude, and you always have them properly planned.

Before we consider the physical differences between the various types of geographical pass (car, couch, doorstep, cinema, etc.) let's go over a few fundamentals.

Should I On the First Date?

This question should never be asked. It's based on an unrealistic assumption about women. Namely, that they act consistently, and as a sex, act the same. They don't. Passes can be made fifteen minutes into a relationship. Passes can be made fifteen dates into a relationship. It all depends on the girl in question.

Petting and Heavy Petting

Two technical terms used by consenting adults to describe the basic form and the escalated form of the initial passionate embrace. Sexual philosophers can often get themselves very uptight over when petting and heavy petting become foreplay – the answers are either twenty-four (when you're desperately trying to shed all the lingering details of your adolescent sexuality, particularly the vocabulary), or when it's followed by penetration. This can be confusing. They are terms which can be used accurately only with hindsight. Kissing someone's neck is petting, but it's also foreplay if it ends in bed.

Males in the front line of sexual activity tend to avoid such euphemisms. It would be rare to find the following conversation:

SCENE: MUSKY PUB, DAY

MALE 1: So anyway, I knew she really fancied me and I thought my luck was in so I started petting her a little.

MALE 2: And then?
MALE 1: Well, you'll never believe it, but she just let me go straight ahead and start heavy petting her.
MALE 2: It sounds great.

It actually sounds like they've been playing with pet rabbits.
The terms are too cutesy. More likely to be as follows:

SCENE: MUSKY PUB, DAY

MALE 1: So anyway, I knew she really fancied me, and I thought my luck was in, so I started having a bit of a ransack.
MALE 2: And then?
MALE 1: Well, she just let me go straight ahead and ransack her completely.
MALE 2: A rape and pillage situation?
MALE 1: At least.

But they can be useful when you're trying to describe accurately what happened to an eager and technically curious friend. Petting is the official term, and so it should be officially understood. Petting starts the moment you start doing something to her which you know you wouldn't do if her mother was in the room. This is a good yardstick. It includes all the small-fry manoeuvres, nuzzling of necks, kissing, rubbing faces, everything, right down to grazing bottoms and touching the breast area on the outside of the clothing. Heavy petting begins the moment you move down to the groin area, or start undoing her clothing and attacking a sexual zone flesh to flesh.

The Base System

The base system is another very straightforward descriptive technique which is a little too American to be really cool, but which has all the accuracy of 'petting' without its prissiness. It's only to be used with younger colleagues,

Sex tip no. 15: The Six Most Important Kisses in the History of the Screen

Like almost everything else the art of the kiss is one which is only perfected with practice. Budding beginners need good role models to copy to get their tongue movements, body positions and passionate glances all up to scratch. And Hollywood is fortunately still providing exceptional examples of all three. The AIDS scare has made some very good technical kissers less open mouthed on the screen but digging into the archives, and including the quite unabashed Richard Gere, does produce five perfect models.

Here they are:

Humphrey Bogart and Lauren Bacall in *The Big Sleep*.
Richard Gere and Debra Winger in *An Officer and a Gentleman*.
Burt Lancaster and Deborah Kerr in *From Here to Eternity*
Clark Gable and Vivian Leigh in *Gone with the Wind*
Christopher Jones and Sarah Miles in *Ryan's Daughter*.

A topical addendum needs to be included with Sylvester Stallone in *Rambo-First Blood Part Two*, when he kisses the Vietnamese girl who's just helped him escape from the POW camp. It's not that this is a particularly good kiss but it is an outstanding one just because it is surrounded by so much blood and guts. The sole moment of saliva in a $30 million bloodbath. Predictably she gets killed in his arms.

---

the under 24s – over that and the exact details of the encounter either aren't required, or are required in such detail that any form of euphemism is useless.

Again they've been made more mysterious than they actually are. Here is the latest base definition from the teenagers hanging out at the Sherman Oaks Galleria in LA. First base is having an initial pass accepted, this means a French kiss and a graze of the breasts (the two now go hand in hand almost universally). Second base is more kissing, a much more determined groping of the breasts, probably on a flesh to flesh basis, and a good deal of stroking. Third base means, quite unequivocally, the groin. Generally it means your hand inside her clothing (external touching around the groin can still be second base). To qualify properly for third base status you need to be touching for about three minutes or more. Fourth base is having sex itself, namely penetration.

The growing popularity of oral sex is something of a complication for the base system as it definitely ranks with penetration and yet is theoretically still an hors d'oeuvre. In terms of sexual gratification blow jobs will often far outstrip straightforward intercourse, but in terms of kudos it still falls behind intercourse. This situation is changing rapidly though. We could see the day dawning when losing your virginity can mean having oral sex as well as intercourse.

Preparing for the Pass

The sheer, unadulterated, flesh-creeping horror of that slight stiffening of the girl's shoulders as you put your arm round her, that slight shifting away to the opposite side of the seat, that long, slow, doleful turning of the head, the concerned, wide-eyed look of commiseration, and then the words, 'Look, I really think we need to talk', are so terrible for the male psyche it is our duty to our sense of self-preservation to avoid them at all costs.

Unfortunately, no matter how many positive signs a girl may be giving you, or how calculated your build-up to that first pass is, you can never be sure whether she's going to accept you until moments before the contact. For that split second, that few inches as your lips motor towards hers, or as your arm curls out over her shoulders, you're taking an enormous leap into the unknown.

However, if you think about a pass in the right way you can at least make it a percentage pass, rather than an instinctive last-minute lunge. It won't necessarily increase your success rate, but it will help you cut down on the direness of the face loss if you get turned down.

What you should do

Vigilance is the key word. Throughout the course of the date you should be firing little mini-passes and watching her reaction closely. A mini-pass is any form of intimate physical contact. As you speak or make a point, touch her on the forearm, describe things and then touch her in the appropriate places as you describe them.

For example:

MALE: You wouldn't believe the weird make-up the mummies in the museum had. It was all drawn back along the eyes here (he touches her temple)

etc. . . .

Any topic of conversation which involves lifting or looking at her hand is a great toe in the tub technique. Men who know a little about palmistry are always using it to provoke fairly extended periods of hand contact while they talk about life lines and fate marks. Mug up on it a bit. If that doesn't appeal find something to say about hands in general. It doesn't really matter that it's a cliché because the girl will probably see through the technique anyway. What you're gauging isn't her interest in the topic of hands, but her reaction to you holding hers. Long gazes into your eyes, a completely relaxed hand in yours, a good deal of laughter are all positive signs.

Hands are good targets for this sort of exploratory attention because they're both neutral and intimate. But the same goes for hair, arms in general, shoulders and faces. Legs and obviously breasts and bottoms are best left alone. Even jokes about them smack a little too much of the lascivious and the crude. Try and be gentle and sophisticated, with overtones of immense confidence, rather than veering between the boorish and the neurotic.

Footsie

Playing footsie is a mildly overrated pastime. Sometimes it sounds great, and in *Flashdance* when Jennifer Beals pushed her feet into her lover's groin ON THEIR FIRST DATE, it looked great too. But generally it's very difficult to tell anything by it. The thing is that footsie isn't about actually rubbing feet frantically up and down calves, at least rarely. It's about almost accidentally touching your foot or leg against hers, then leaving it there and seeing what she does. If she just leaves hers then you gradually push a bit closer, and see what reaction a little more pressure gets. You've got to keep the above board conversation going throughout all this, and if you're attacking with your feet it's as well to ease off with the hands or else your partner might feel a little hemmed in. Nine times out of ten though, if her leg doesn't move it's because she hasn't thought about it, so while you're getting all excited she's given absolutely no signals. The moment she senses it she moves away, leading you to chase her feet around the carpet for a bit and then assume she's just playing hard to get.

The Timing of the Pass

If you've met her at eight, by about ten-thirty, you'll be thinking about taking the evening to its next stage. The next half-hour is statistically speaking, the best for making a pass. In a study at a cinema in Enciro, CA, 70 per cent of passes made in this two and a half hours were accepted. It's late enough to be romantic and hidden, it's early enough to mean that all those begged questions about nightcaps, last buses and sleeping arrangements are still fairly distant. It's the perfect time to strike.

The very best general, semi-pass technique, a technique

which virtually guarantees you an answer as to whether she likes you or not, and yet which limits your face-on-the-line commitment is the linking arms method.

Rather than grabbing her hand, or helping her on with her coat and then trying to leave your arm over her shoulder, or even worse, looking at her long and hard and then moving forward lips puckered, in a major kiss attempt, just link arms. It's always a good idea to have a short walk after the principal date activity is over, and before the hoped-for sexual activity begins, and it's an excellent no man's land to try the exploratory shot which will pave the way for the full-scale pass later.

As you begin to walk along together, away from the cinema or restaurant, you on the outside (ever the gentleman) just hold out your arm, hand still in its pocket, so that she can take it. If she laughs nervously and doesn't, it's going to hurt like hell, because the chances are she's not interested, but at least you haven't lunged passionately. If she takes it, however, you get that wonderful feeling of elation and self-satisfaction tingling all up and down your body because you can be almost certain that she will be on for something later on. The beauty of the method is that you can explore further so easily.

Notice how closely she holds on to you. Pull your elbow in a bit further and see whether she comes. If all is going well you can slip your arm round her shoulders as the next stage and take it from there.

Obviously if you're confident about the signs you've been getting in the course of the evening, or else are completely confused by her behaviour, you can go straight for the pass. But the sting of a refusal is always so terrible that a brief linking of arms really is no great hardship considering the pain it could be saving you from.

The Arm Across Her Shoulder

The arm around the shoulders is really the most widely acknowledged major first pass. Going straight in for a kiss is almost too foolhardy for there to be any sympathy for the victim of a rejection – if you're that confident go for it, but no matter what it's never a percentage pass. The arm on the shoulders is a universally understood gesture. If the girl accepts it, she has accepted your initial intentions. Keep the arm fairly relaxed, not a bar of flexed bone rigid with nervous tension, balanced on her shoulder blades. A good, natural, relaxed arm across, or arm over (the first stage of the leg over) is actually fairly bent, the crook of your elbow around the back of her neck, your hand resting near her face. If this goes well you can then stroke her face a little, then her ear and her hair as you build up for the first kiss. Remember that all this initial passing is occurring on that crucial walk just after the activity has finished and the going home stage is about to begin.

It should be noted that some men feel dates imply by their very nature that a pass should be made during their principal activity. Take going to the cinema, they say. The girl will begin to think you're a wimp if you don't move during the film.

The answer to this is that it's a valid point under the age of nineteen, over that, and out of adolescence, everyone's beginning to take themselves more seriously as 'complete human beings', rather than targets for sexual advances. Putting your arm round a lower sixth former's shoulders in the Penge Odeon on a Friday night is one thing. Putting it round a senior marketing consultant is quite different. Keep to the linked arms for more mature dates, and for all unpredictable ones.

The First Kiss

One of the biggest controversies still raging in the area of the first kiss is whether you should ask permission.

The pro-permissioners' point is, easy to grasp. According to them, asking a girl for permission is to treat her as a civilized human being, to give her a civilized opportunity to say what she actually thinks. There are no 'ifs' or 'buts', or attempts to decipher the notoriously vague and misleading phrases of body language that have danced mistily before the anxious male's eyes all through the date. He gets an absolutely bell-clear answer. In addition, the permissioners argue, coming boldly out with the question, without a trace of a quiver in your voice, helps the girl feel confident about you. You appear calm, self-assured, in control, and this all helps her relax and succumb.

The doers say this is a technique for wimps. These born-again Hemingways believe in action, not words. They handle passes, and sex in general, the way he handled words, they keep it short and to the point. They act on gut feeling. They look the girl in the eyes, then try and plant one of her lips. Asking permission, they say, is to hold up a placard saying. 'I'm too nervous to do it, please say it's okay', and they equate nerves with bad breath and dandruff as a pollutant to sexual chemistry.

In fact a middle way does exist. The doers do have a point. Wimpishness and nerves can be great destroyers of sexual advance unless the girl is the mother type. However, well-controlled nerves and the right sort of question can be really effective.

The right way to ask

SCENE: CAR, NIGHT

MAN: Look, I've got to admit that I'm sitting here now, trying to decide whether I should kiss you or not.
GIRL: Oh, Charles. (*She melts into his arms.*)

Asking honestly does seem to work.

Asking over-politely, or over-confidently on the other hand either appears wimpish, or plain rude. A confident question makes it sound like you're expecting a yes, and have been all along, or even worse that she says yes all the time. It deprives her of her mystery (girls like mystery). A polite question makes it sound like the right to taste her lips is no more special than the right to ask for the salt at the table.

Wrong way to ask – CONFIDENT

MAN: Hey, Jane, howsabout a kiss then?
WOMAN: It's late, I really must be going.

Wrong – POLITE

MAN: Jane, may I give you a kiss, please?
WOMAN: Look, Charles, I think it's time we talked.

The kiss itself would seem to be the acid test of whether she wants you or not. But it's wrong to think of 'the first kiss' in the singular. It never hurts to be too cautious. Remember how much it hurts to be rejected. What some lovers will do is try and break up this first kiss so that by the time lip-to-lip contact is about to be made, smaller scale kisses in more neutral spots have already been delivered and accepted. In other words, they nuzzle a bit before a major pass. This isn't wet nuzzling, in the sense of soppy and wimpish – it's cool, calculated, sophisticated nuzzling.

This really is very easy once your arms are linked, or your arm is across her shoulders. As you walk you have been occasionally pulling her a little closer, testing the degree of her inertia, letting her out again. If it's all going well on the next pull in you can try whispering something in her ear. Don't make it too romantic or passionate. Keep it mildly humorous, but very nice. Then do the same again but keeping your face closer to hers this time, resting your cheek on hers, slightly grazing your lips across it as you pull away. Then just keep this up. Giving her occasional little grazes. If she really isn't interested she'll put a stop to this immediately. If she doesn't mind the chances are that she'll definitely go for the main pass. Also it's worth noting that brushing kisses around ears and necks can be very provocative to a lot of girls, actually getting them as interested in more heavy breathing activity as fast as the lip-to-lip series.

The Main Kiss

Suddenly you know it's time to launch the main kiss. You can see it in her eyes that she's waiting for you to make a move, and you can also see that she isn't giving you any more clues. You have to commit yourself. With girls you always have to take some sort of a leap into the darkness no matter how encouraging they are, or how observant you've been. The key with kissing is to keep it simple, especially on the first one.

Don't try and do it too slowly to start off with, licking lips, sucking teeth, concentrating on advanced open-mouth flourishes. Keep these for later. Just make the first kiss a basic, gentle, French kiss. Lips touch, tongue enters, waggles around slowly for a bit, then draws away and pauses for a moment.

You can now catch your breath and prepare to plunge in seriously.

The symbolic offer and acceptance is now over. The worst mistake you can make is to blast away at the first kiss too passionately. This can be far too intimidating. Remember you're about to put your tongue in a complete stranger's mouth. You need to do it slowly and politely. If she jumps on you when you do it, then of course it's okay to respond, but as long as you're leading, start slowly.

Eyes open or eyes closed?

Immediately, another issue comes up. Should you kiss with eyes open or closed? On films, of course, all lovers

Sex tip no. 16: Does 'No' Really Mean 'Yes'?

'When a girl says "no" she really means "yes".' This is another of sex's greatest clichés and needs a little closer examination.

In fact when girls say no they don't mean yes any more or less than boys do. The key here is to listen to how she says no.

Let's take a look at the classic refusal of a pass.

GIRL: Oh, God, look at the time, I really must be going.

This is a real 'no'. She really MUST be going. There is no room to negotiate on this word. It's a decision she's already made. Gripping her shoulder more tightly, or pushing harder won't make her succumb. You'll end up slapped or in court.

However, this answer is different.

GIRL: Oh, look at the time, I really should be going.

Here opportunity is still beckoning hard. She knows it's late, she's nervous, but she hasn't decided yet. 'Shoulds' need to be attacked. Now's the time to stop those synapses firing. Thought has a way of being uncontrollably bourgeois, give it long enough and it will always decide it should really go home early and read. You need to push forward the advances and let the hormones take over. She obviously likes you or she'd have said 'must'.

---

have their eyes shut the moment the lips touch, the girl's often for longer. Now for girls it's no problem. They are essentially having this done to them and being in the passenger seat they don't need to see what's going on. For the male, keeping a good bearing is vital, especially as the kissing generally starts late at night, when he's tired, and in a dark place.

Basically it's more stylish to kiss with eyes closed but

many men feel that it's too much of a waste to work and worry that much for something, and then when it finally comes, not to watch it. And of course it's no problem anyway as long as the girl is keeping her eyes closed. The problem comes if she suddenly opens them in mid-kiss. Immediately you feel stupid, as if you've been caught out looking. In this instance don't shut your eyes quickly. This is a complete giveaway and actually makes you look guilty. Instead, sort of melt your features, as if overcome by emotion, and hug tighter. Often the girl will then shut her eyes again.

Shutting eyes does have certain very distinct advantages, one in particular pointed out by many girls, which is you can pretend it's someone else much more easily.

The History of the French Kiss

Rumour has it that the French kiss was originally the Flu kiss, a kiss conceived about one thousand years ago when the first flu virus floated into Northern France and started blocking people's noses. Some way had to be found of keeping up the kissing despite the blocked noses and aching limbs. Well, the obvious answer was to open your mouth during the kiss. This let you breathe, and your tongue could start doing the walking instead of the desperately aching fingers and hands. The result seemed to please everyone, and when the virus retreated in the face of warmer weather and throat lozenges, they kept the style on. In no time at all 'Norman' kissing, had become 'French flu kissing' and finally plain French kissing.

But with this major sexual discovery came a problem previously unencountered.

Dribbling

Kissing with your mouth open means indefinitely postponing the regular swallows which siphon off the saliva build-up. In a prolonged French kiss there comes a point when there is simply too much liquid draining forward through your teeth. The drainage operation is definitely the male's responsibility because he is generally taller, he is looking down at the girl, which means his saliva is charging at her. You can't swallow, because it's virtually impossible to swallow with your mouth open, unless you pull your tongue back and tighten all your throat muscles. And this doesn't feel nice for the girl being kissed. At the same time, you can't let it run all over her face.

There is, however, a polite way to avoid all this unpleasantness. It consists of waiting until the saliva has built up to an unbearable degree, and then gradually raising your head till it's level, very quickly drawing your breath in as you do so. This starts hoovering in the liquid. At the end of the kiss you scoop your head round to one side, drawing down her lips to remove the last drops. The move completed, you swallow and start again. It's important only to draw your breath in, not to suck it. The latter makes far too much noise and feels decidedly strange.

Petting: The Breast

Bearing in mind the crucial point about keeping the kiss going, your next target is likely to be the breast (also known as the tit, the boob, the Bristol and the zard). Sometimes it's hard to judge how long you should wait before tracing your hand down the front of her clothing, and there really is no fixed permitted period. Some girls respond very quickly, others not so quickly. But very generally speaking if you're still French kissing away with a moderately enthusiastic response after one minute, you should be thinking in terms of breasts.

Before zeroing straight in on the target it's a good idea to let your hands roam around a bit, avoiding the groin and inner thigh, but grazing the outer thigh, the stomach and the arms. On the way back up let it brush over a breast and notice the response.

Obviously any sign of an erect nipple is helpful but these are notoriously difficult to find at any time of the day, under layers of clothing, and even more so at night. Anyway, if the response seems neutral, or positive, take your hand back down again and pay a little more attention.

The cardinal error at this point, and the most frequent, is to attack the helpless mammary in its lace and elastic cage with too much gusto. Too often the overwhelming sense of relief and rising tide of passion that greets the acceptance of that first brush turns into a brutal pounding of the unsuspecting breast. This really hurts and kills the passion dead. Be gentle with it to start with and only build up the pressure if the owner's reaction becomes more enthusiastic.

Sex tip no. 17: Breasts

The naïve simplicity of the male's conviction that the female breast's willing to respond to his fumbling touch is as touching as it is misplaced. Many breasts and nipples are extremely fond of being handled by male hands, the owner writhes with unconcealed delight when it happens, they are like mini-erections with minds of their own. But breasts are far more variable, and more moody in their sexual response than erections. Some are very excitable, but others just don't give a damn. If you've been pumping away at one of these for a while, just give in: they've probably gone numb, after all. Don't try and be the first to breathe sexual life into the stern nipples. No sexual heroics, or sensual artistry will be enough to get through. Just leave them and stop making a fool of yourself. It's a lost cause.

If she says no

Provided you've got a full French kiss in, a clamped female hand firmly pulling yours away from the breast area is not necessarily a complete 'no'. The old 'no means yes' rule doesn't really hold water except in very early, light petting. Elsewhere it has to be handled very carefully.

If she removes your hand once, it could be just good manners, the sexual equivalent of saying no to seconds.

Try again very gingerly, a few seconds later. If she says no twice, it could be obstinacy or shyness, a little more depressing but you can still respectably get away with a third attempt. If she removes it again you MUST stop trying. Further attempts smack too much of chest hair, gold chains and white socks.

What to do if you suddenly don't fancy her

Just as girls can easily be turned off by that first kiss, even after fancying and fantasizing about the kisser intensely for weeks, so it can happen to you too. Sometimes you realize as you lift your head and she follows with hers, suddenly offering her lips and inviting you and your tongue inside, that you don't really want to go. The buzz is all from knowing you can do it. When you've got that, you don't actually want to do it. This isn't a good habit to get into. There isn't a word for the male version of a cock-teaser but you get a reputation fast and there's just as much bad feeling about them. But when it happens, how do you get out of it? Well, it's like getting out of an invite that you've already RSVP'd to. Basically you've got two choices. You can either go for a watered-down kiss, and then explain your way out of another date at a later stage and on the telephone.

Or you can avoid the kiss completely and take the painful consequences of her disappointment now. Current fashion favours the watered-down kiss. The watered-down kiss means keeping your lips closed, grazing hers for a bit, then slipping into a long hug. Long hugs are actually more

Sex tip no. 18: Bra Straps

According to teenage myth, every male under the age of eighteen thinks about sex once every sixteen seconds, and how to undo bra straps once every twenty-five.

This is a complete fallacy. Bra straps never really need to be undone at the petting stage, and at the full home base stage the girl will probably take it off herself anyway.

No, you don't need to worry about whether it's a back-fastener, a front loader, a velcro strap or anything. As long as you can unbutton the first few buttons of her shirt or blouse and slide your hand down to her shoulder, you're away. Normally the female shoulder will rise up as you slide (because it tickles) and then it's easy just to push the strap off the top of the shoulder. This loosens all the tension in the cup and lets you slip your hand inside.

It's worth noting that hand to breast contact beneath clothes remains petting. Heavy petting is confined to the groin area.

---

emotional than sexual, so they avoid the issue. It does mean that the evening ends unresolved, but it allows you to stall for time, decide if you really don't want the girl, and then work out how to drop her on the phone rather than in mid-date.

Escalating the Engagement

Going into third base, the groin area, is really the big move, and unfortunately the girls know this too. This is the sexual equivalent of a conventional war going nuclear. You're in that no man's land where petting ends and heavy petting begins. If you're lucky your partner will be getting so excited that there really isn't any question of whether you should or shouldn't. Unfortunately though, everyone's awareness of this move's significance siphons out natural progressions. A sexual stalemate is reached with the girl waiting, sphinx-like for your move, and you desperate to do it but unable to tell whether she wants it yet or not.

Terrible no-win situations flicker through your mind's eye. Recognize one of these and you will be familiar with the state known as 'loss of sexual bottle'.

GIRL (*writhing, slightly stale now after several minutes' of breast attention*): Oh, Richard, mmmh.
RICHARD (*kneading away stoically but knowing it's time*): Mmmmh, Diana, mmmh.
ERECTION: If you don't move down now she'll think you're a wimp. She'll tell her friends that you're scared to do it. She'll think you don't know what to do.
EGO (over): But she kept saying over dinner that she had to get home early, that might have been a warning. And what about that 'friend' at work, you know, the bodybuilder, she kept on mentioning him, I think that's a boyfriend. And remember how slowly she kissed you at first. I think she's unsure.
ERECTION: Get your hand down.
EGO: Wait till tomorrow.
GIRL: Mmmh, Richard.
ERECTION: GET YOUR HAND DOWN.
EGO: SHE'LL SLAP YOU IN THE FACE.
GIRL: Mmmmh, mmmh, Richard.
RICHARD: Oh shit.

The result can often be long French kisses with you absent-mindedly kneading her breasts, your brain filled with an almost overwhelming desire to move on down, but the whole thing checked by that black fear of being stopped. Nothing in the whole world feels more terrible than that sudden vice-like grip on your arm as it slides up her thigh. The breast block is bad, but the groin block is somehow worse because you've been led to believe that you're in line for so much more.

What to do after the block

Don't try and wrench your arm out of her hand and plunge defiantly downwards in the hope that she'll get over her shyness. Notice how she blocks your advance. If she replaces you back on her breasts you know that she's still interested but is making a symbolic point. She's letting you know that she isn't the sort of girl who lets men go down this fast. In this event your confidence can remain high. At some point in the not too distant future she will give in and you're perfectly entitled to another stab at the forbidden zone on that date.

If she blocks you and then breaks off the embrace altogether and starts straightening her clothes, you know you're in trouble. This isn't symbolic. This is pissed off. She's decided you've gone too far and is angry.

Whatever happens don't let the date end without some more contact, hopefully lip to lip, otherwise the whole thing's doomed. Leave everything for a moment, let the tension and your erection relax, switch from attack to defence. You're saving face now. Don't say, 'Look, can we talk about it', or 'Oh, God, I'm really sorry, you probably think I don't respect you now'. This worked in the fifties (what happy times those must have been) but dramatically doesn't today.

For years girls seemed ready to believe that men whose whole bodies were throbbing with the desire to bend them over chairs and put erections in their mouths were essentially preoccupied with respecting them as whole human beings. Gradually they discovered that a rampant erection only has room for one type of thought. Dirty ones. Shared interests, good conversation, a slowly forged trust and affection are like the man in the moon to the erection's cave-man mind. No, the female sex basically understands the psychology of the erection (if not the physical dynamics) much too well nowadays for any verbal explanations, excuses or pleadings to be effective. You have to inject some calm and then let the whole thing subside until it feels right to make the pass again.

Bottoms

Bottoms are very nice things to touch. The fact that one spends so much time touching one's own is adequate evidence of this. Girls' bottoms are even nicer. But the thing about them is that they are a relatively neutral zone, at least compared to the groin, and yet fairly close to it. Look at it in purely geographical terms. When you're stroking around in the mid-bottom area you're a matter of no more than two or three inches away from the vagina. This is amazingly close. All the frontal assault areas that near are firmly covered with pubic hair, and nothing covered with pubic hair, or six inches from it, is ever neutral. It's base three or more. So if you're really uncertain of the big steps from the breasts, hold on and move for the bottom. If you're accepted, you're close enough to see the attack home very quickly. If you're turned down it's not the same complete loss of face that comes with a groin rejection. Losing on a lesser target costs less face.

Getting to the groin successfully

If you get down to the groin successfully you know you're really accepted. This relationship is very likely to go the whole way. But you need to do the right thing with what's down there. The problem for most males is that they have never had the chance to get properly acquainted with the exact anatomy of the region. Even close study of dirty magazines fails to reveal anything really consistent that could act as a sort of sexual ordnance survey. They all look different. Where does the bottom end and the vagina start? Do they part in the middle or at the side? What are all those folds of skin? Where is the clitoris? What do you do with it?

The essentially baffling geography of the region isn't helped by the fact that men are expected to get to know it generally in the dark, often with the wrong hand, bent round at an angle, in an extreme state of physical arousal, in the back seat of a car or cinema. The result can be a seriously flawed mental picture of the target.

Let's take it slowly.

The vagina and the clitoris

There are two broad philosophies dealing with treatment of the female groin. The first is the purist vein. This asserts that the only really important section is the clitoris, that elusive little button which is responsible for the vast majority of female orgasms. The second is the more practical. It says you should thrash away at the whole thing because it's all pretty sensitive and there's always the possibility that you'll stumble across the clitoris in the course of your groping.

The latter is the more popular because of the overwhelmingly frustrating tendency of the clitoris to move around. The thing about the clitoris is that it's essentially nomadic. You can sleep with the same girl every day for a year and each time you go looking for it, it will be in a different place. It sounds stupid because by the looks of it there's just not that many places it could feasibly go. But it finds all sorts of nooks and crannies. It dodges into little vaginal backwaters, dives into folds of skin, it behaves like it's trying to make you look incompetent. To confound your index finger even more, it can also change shape and texture, growing bigger and then suddenly shrinking again. The results can be very disconcerting. Much as you might

---

Sex tip no. 19: Getting Stuck Inside

If you're having sex with a girl and she's about to cough, get out fast. The same applies if she's about to laugh. Both conditions can lead to a sudden contraction of all the vaginal muscles which translates into a fantastic amount of pressure clamped around the penis. This is mortifyingly painful and more of a turn-off than saltpetre.

---

like to keep one hand roaming around her breasts or the bottom while your good hand concentrates on romancing her clitoris, this is an extremely difficult thing to master. Rather like patting your head and rubbing your tummy. What tends to happen is that a moment is reached when the man is hunting for the clitoris, using all his attention and energy on locating it, and the girl is just lying back, waiting for him to find it.

It's a bit like defusing a bomb, only in reverse. Your date will implode, fall in on itself, if you don't discover the hidden clitoris before all the passion has washed away. You have to move fast and firmly. This is the problem of committing yourself to attacking the clitoris and the clitoris alone. The girl will know what you're after, and will be lying back waiting.

If you don't find it, what do you do? Go back to rubbing her breasts?

That's why it's better to attack the whole vagina, then if you do miss the clitoris at least you've got the rest of the vagina to carry on dealing with.

How to attack it

The technique most widely favoured in Western Europe is the Scout's Honour technique, so named because it involves the second or middle finger on each hand (the principal digit in the Scout's Honour signal). Hold your hand up in front of you for a moment, fingers together. The importance of the middle finger in clitoral search and destroy missions is obvious. It's very long. Your writing hand is generally the most sensitive and you need to start thinking about what side to attack from. If you're right-handed, it's best to attack from the right so that you can reach over and move in from the front, with plenty of leverage. Attacking from the left right-handed is extremely difficult, sometimes involving turning your back on your partner and pushing the finger at her elbow first.

Left-handers attack from the left.

This favours the right-handed male drivers in left-hand

Sex tip no. 20: Making a Noise

Many men feel embarrassed of showing they're getting quite excited. Girls don't have this problem. As long as you're not physically hurting them, they make no bones about the fact that they're enjoying what's going on. It's important to get over the feeling of foolishness if you give the odd 'uhh huhh', because these sorts of noises during sex can make it all feel a lot better. They turn you on and your partner. Practise a bit next time you masturbate, not too loudly, just audibly and quickly.

The rock hard, unmoved, Richard Gere, love machine mode is admittedly cool, but it restricts your fun. It makes you look serious, and after a bit you start feeling serious.

---

drive countries. In America, ironically, the land of all that's starred, striped, and macho, it's better to be driven by a girl if you're a right-hander.

There are times when you're going to have to use your bad hand. On these occasions it's best to be less bold.

Go for general petting rather than precision moves no matter how confident you are. Remember that you can't tell the girl before you start that you're going to be using your bad hand so could she excuse any fumbling that follows. She'll be judging you solely on your performance this time out.

The Scout technique is in fact a relatively modern invention. Obviously it owes a great debt to Lord Baden-Powell and his Youth movement, but it has also been much exploited in popular literature as a prime example of gangland thirties American passion. This is the method that Johnny Fontane uses in Mario Puzo's *The Godfather*.

Its beauty is that it always gives you your bearings, no matter what cramped, dark space you find yourself in, and no matter what shape of girl you're necking with. It's basically a two-move method. You go down the front, with your middle finger pressing lightly, starting on the pubic hair and dropping gently down until you've passed right over the mysterious lumps and folds which make up the vagina, and have come to a small, hard bar. This marks the 'no entry' zone. Beyond this the mystery becomes the bottom, and you need to keep clear. Pause for a moment, and then run it, with a little more pressure, back up the route you've just come along, again fairly slowly. Just before you get to the pubic hair you should notice your partner buck suddenly. The buck marks the spot. This is the clitoris. Carry on over it, and repeat the procedure a few times until you're fairly certain you know where it is. Then have a stab at it on its own. If you lose it, go back to square one and start again.

Having Intercourse

Obviously there's lots of fun and pleasure to be had along the petting way, but intercourse remains the bottom line. There are those trying to suggest that virginity shouldn't be attached so closely to whether you've had intercourse or not, and that lots and lots of petting experience can actually make the final business of slipping it in and out a few times seem rather insignificant. Also, as the woman's lobby has pointed out to the growing paranoia of male lovers everywhere, women often don't have orgasms during intercourse, and are far more likely to have theirs during foreplay. But we all know that despite all that when it comes down to it intercourse remains the Real Thing. Oral sex and Pepsi can try all they like, it won't make any difference. The fact that one finds it so hard to know what to call it is an adequate illustration of its importance.

Do you call it having sex, making love, having intercourse, fucking, screwing, getting laid, banging, going all the way, slipping into something more comfortable? This is really a hard one. When you're with a girl, you'll want to use an expression which sounds sympathetic and sensitive as well as passionate.

This rules out, 'Do you wanna fuck?' 'Do you wanna screw?' and 'Do you wanna get laid?' 'Do you want to have intercourse?' makes you sound like a doctor or a mechanic ('Do you want your oil changed or your blood pressure taken?'). 'Do you want to make love?' sounds about the best but seems a little incongruous if you only met her a couple of hours ago, or you're thrashing around in the front of your car. Also with passions up, and emotions exposed, people can get very sensitive about the words you use, and remember them. They can and will be used in evidence against you at a later date. Refer to your getting off as 'making love', and your partner might assume your level of involvement and commitment is higher than it actually is. Do you want to have sex? is about all that's left, a compromise, albeit an accurate one. But it's too surgical to whisper in someone's ear, or breathe over a nightcap.

The ideal is to avoid having to ask altogether. But given that there will be occasions when you *can't* avoid it, what are you left with?

Answer: The clichés.

Where did you think all those 'Let's spend the night together', 'I just want to be so much closer to you', 'Shall I slip into something more comfortable?' lines came from? Desperate human beings trying to find a way of saying or asking the unaskable. The best and cleanest of all is, 'Would you like me to stay?' It wraps everything up in such a neutral little grey verb, 'staying'. And it lets her answer, 'Would you like to stay?' if she's still determined to let you do the leading and the risking.

MALE: Gosh, I'm really tired, oh god, look at the time, (*yawns*) I'm really tired.

FEMALE: Yes, I suppose I should be going to bed really.

MALE: Mmm. Look do you think it would be all right if I stayed here on the sofa. I just don't know if I can face driving back.

This is the other gambit, the 'find any way of staying somewhere near her bedroom' ploy. Remember that it doesn't matter where she lets you stay in her flat. As long as you're under the same roof for the night your chances are very high. The great thing about staying on sofas or floors is that when you're both finished in the bathroom you will inevitably go in and say goodnight. She'll be undressed, in bed, and thinking about the date gone by. Ninety per cent of goodnight kisses end in spermicidal jelly in these situations.

But whatever happens, if you are allowed to stay in some neutral place in her flat, and the goodnight kiss doesn't work as well as planned, don't go into a 'sleep but not touch' conversation. This is the worst sort of sexual shop steward bargaining, and is too tawdry for words, let alone sex.

MALE: Look, I know, why don't I slip into your bed, but we'll put the pillows down the middle so that we don't do anything we didn't mean to in the night. I wouldn't ask, it's just that my back's a little sore from playing squash.

FEMALE: No, really, I think you'll be fine on the sofa.

MALE: Actually, I've got a better idea, why don't I put my head down the other end of the bed, and my feet at your end. There'll be no danger, really.

FEMALE: Really, the sofa will be much more comfortable.

MALE (*pleading now*): Oh, look, don't you understand? I just want to be close to you. I'm not thinking about sex, I just want to be near you.

FEMALE: I'll call you a taxi.

Different Places to Make Passes

The best place to make a pass is one which allows you to lie down as soon as possible after starting the physical contact. Once you're well into base 3, base 4 is really looming large and the faster things are allowed to escalate, the better.

Of course the problem is that most first passes are made outside flats and houses, often in the most inhospitable of conditions. In cars you can actually have sex but it's always rather difficult, and the mess is so annoying. The problem is that you can't get all your clothes off so in the tussles that ensue, they suffer. The result is great wedges of sperm all over your jacket or trouser leg which have to be explained away as yoghurt stains because they never dry clean out. Most car sex now takes place in front rather than back seats. This is probably something to do with the population growth.

In the fifties, when car sex really took off it was so much easier to find deserted roads and so climb into the back seat of your car and really get down to some serious undressing and intercourse. Nowadays, unless you live in the countryside, it's really hard to find a completely deserted street. Even at two in the morning you can drive around for hours trying to find somewhere not lit up by 4000-watt street lamps or paced by late-night walkers. The result is a feeling of unease. You're always expecting to have to break off any moment, and look as if you're sitting having a chat or trying to find something in the *A-Z*. And of course it's terribly difficult to look normal with your clothes off, an erection on, and both of you sitting in the back seat of the car. Take the other option and just get down as low as you can, so low that you can't be seen, and then run the risk and the tremendous embarrassment of having to cope with someone breaking into your car. Then what do you do? Sit up and tell them to stop? It's altogether too hard.

Another thing about cars is that with the energy crisis and the Japanese, the small, sporty car has taken over in popularity from the big cruisers. Big cruisers are excellent for having sex in. They're like king sizes on wheels.

Two sorts of cars have traditionally always been the

Sex tip no. 21: Do Girls Talk About Your Performance to Friends?

Everyone has that horrible feeling that if you've just made an idiot of yourself on a date, bungled a pass, been slapped, been turned down, the girl has rushed off the next day and started telling all her friends about it. For a few weeks you get that ghastly nauseous embarrassment when you see anyone that knows her well at parties, and they seem to be looking at you too long and too curiously.

You're sure they're laughing at you, that they know every appalling detail of your premature ejaculation in the car or whatever your sin against petting actually was. But do girls really rush away and talk to their friends about you? Have you really got anything to worry about or is it all in your mind? The answer, unfortunately, is keep worrying. Men have no monopoly on sexual gossip or lurid detail. Women love it too.

---

hardest to have sex in – sports cars, and small cars. Small cars have the most obvious drawbacks, but add the basic problems of the sports car, bucket seats (impossible to get out of, or into), sucked in bodywork, low roof, fat gear stick, and you've got real trouble. Necking in these is really hard.

If you're really intent on going through with it in a car, the passenger seat is the way to go, generally with the man underneath. Girls tend to be smaller and can operate in the reduced space to more effect. 'Yoghurt stains' are virtually guaranteed, though.

CINEMAS are actually very easy places to make passes in, at least initially. The seats are designed for arms to rest along the back and gradually be rolled down onto the shoulders of girls sitting in them. You'll also notice that the curve of the seats and the curve of the rows, combined with the darkness, makes it very hard to see what's going on in neighbouring seats.

This protects you from prying eyes. The main danger is in the height of the seats. Newer cinemas are not so high backed, so the arm around the back manoeuvre isn't so obvious, but the older ones, with the large wooden backs are tricky. You really have to lift your arm up to get it in place. This both attracts the attention of those sitting behind you, and means your elbow comes dangerously close to your partner's face.

The main thing is to keep the whole movement slow and controlled. This makes it less noticeable and reduces the damage you're likely to inflict should you hit your partner with your elbow. Slow-moving elbows hurt less.

One French Girl's Thoughts on the First Kiss and Heavy Petting

'The kiss should suggest what's going to come later – it should be soft and moist, with blasts of hard and precise mixed in. You've got to show you can be gentle, and that you can dominate too. The girl doesn't want to show how she does it, she wants to lie back and let you do it. She wants to see what you're like, and then decide

(a) if you're any good at it
(b) what role to play herself (innocent virgin, experienced older woman.

A lot of girls will wait until that first kiss to decide whether they're going to sleep with a man or not. It's not always because they can't make up their mind from the way he looks and talks. It's the same procedure with men that they really like. Somehow the way a man does that first kiss can be so good but also so off-putting. If it's really bad no matter what they look like you just go right off them.'

The kiss is therefore to relax the girl, to soothe her

doubts, and to set the scene. It mustn't be jerky, it must flow. The man must not give the girl time to think. If he does the same thing time and time again she will get bored. Her mind will wander, and she'll suddenly seize up. Above all he must use his hands at the same time.

If you're not sure whether you can stroke breasts this early then use them on the back of the girl's neck, her hair, her face. This actually gives the girl lots of confidence. If you leave them dangling by your side because you're not sure what you'll be allowed to do yet she'll start wondering what you're up to, where your hands actually are, whether they're suddenly going to appear on her thigh at any moment. Use your hands too, on her shoulders and back, but be careful not to do it too hard on her back, otherwise you'll pull her shirt or blouse up from her skirt or trousers and she'll start to panic.

Girls' panic

The girl's panic isn't always, 'Oh god I don't want it to go this far', but very often, 'I hope that my underwear looks all right'. Some girls, when they're out on an early date with a man they really fancy and know they will probably succumb to too fast under normal circumstances, will wear their oldest, most unattractive underwear on the date so that they know they'll be able to pull back in the event of everything going too far for propriety. He'd be so shocked by the ugliness of it all that he'd probably never speak to her again. So you don't necessarily have to worry if she seems hesitant. This doesn't mean making a full frontal assault, no matter what she says or does. It does mean keeping up continuous contact, gradually getting bolder. If you keep kissing and stroking a girl enough, her body will start asking for more.

Sex tip no. 22: Should You or Shouldn't You On a First Date?

This depends entirely on the girl. If you've got to base 3 on date one, the chances are you can if you want to, and she'll let you know. If you get a passionate kiss on the doorstep this is a no. You can suggest coffee if you like, but she will definitely have thought the situation over and decided one way or the other. You can push once, but make it as light as possible.

CAROLINE (*firmly after the kiss*): Thank you for a wonderful evening.

HENRY (*smiling*): Can you really leave me, cold, tired, and alone, left to face the night and the roads without even a cup of coffee?

It's corny, but she knows you're asking, and she also sees you're being relaxed so that if she says 'no', it won't be a major loss of face for you in her eyes. You won't have appeared to have gone out on a limb.

If she does invite you up, the necking will inevitably start again and you'll be moving rapidly towards the CONTRACEPTIVE BREAK.

A French Girl's View of Petting

'The most difficult thing for a girl in a petting situation is knowing when to put her hand on a man's penis. You see a girl has to go straight from kissing to touching the penis, and that's a big jump. If the man starts rubbing it against her in a sort of fairly general way, just enough so that she can feel it through his trousers, that's a great help because it sort of introduces it into the play of things. NEVER, though, whatever happens, take a girl's hand and put it on your penis. This makes her feel terrible, as if you've been waiting for her to do it for hours and that she's been so naïve or insensitive that she hasn't realized. Rub it on her gently, then she'll take over.'

CHAPTER 6

Contraception

This chapter should definitely begin with a disclaimer. All of the advice it gives and dangers it lists only apply to accidental and unwanted pregnancies. If you're longing to be a father, or to make the girl a mother, or else the whole thing is just a delightful surprise, then great. You won't have these angsts. If you're not ready for parenthood yet, this chapter's for you.

Let's assume, though, that you either get asked up or the goodnight kiss on the sofa worked, and things are moving full steam ahead. You MUST, whatever happens, stop for a CONTRACEPTIVE BREAK.

In the bath, at the rugby club, at the bar around a pint with your arm across your best friend's beer belly, it's a macho truism that 'getting a girl into trouble' is her trouble. That's why it's a laugh. Contraception is the girl's responsibility, runs the macho logic, just like shaving is the man's.

This, however, is a dangerous creed. Unusually, for the school of machismo and medallionism, it's a creed with logic behind it. It's definitely in the girl's interest not to get pregnant; if the shit does hit the fan, the fan is after all, pointing right at her. But girls are just strange on this issue.

Question them, coldly, over a pizza, and they'll tell you things about IUDs, temperature methods, and the Pope that'll turn your mind inside out. They really know about birth control. But in the heat of the moment this has a tendency to go out of the window. First, there's the moral issue. In the shadow of the time-honoured good-girl stereotype it's better for a girl not to plan to have sex with a date, and so not to take any precautions and then give in at the last moment, than it is to come prepared. Giving in, and getting pregnant, is only murder two. Premeditated contraception is murder one, even though it's free of morning sickness.

Second, girls are just so cavalier about missing periods, forgetting to take the Pill, having holes in their diaphragms, having sheaths burst on them.

MALE (*slightly nervous*): When's your next period due?
FEMALE (*casually*): Last week some time.
MALE (*anxiously*): Do you normally miss?
GIRL (*casually*): Hardly ever. Oooh, I really feel sick.
MALE (*slightly afraid, looking at his watch, realizing it's the morning*): You have been wearing your diaphragm?
FEMALE (*casually*): Oh yes. Actually, I've got to get a new one. You know I really feel quite sick.
MALE (*very afraid now*): Why a new diaphragm?
FEMALE (*casually*): I noticed some holes in the old one.
MALE (*nauseously*): Oh.

And third, there comes a point when women go a little funny about having children. Somewhere about twenty-five to twenty-six they start getting broody. Mix this in with a dash of 'one-parent family liberationism' and you've got a dangerous situation. She might try and get pregnant by you, and not tell you she's doing it.

Forget the macho, 'don't give a damn code', forget the bathroom attempts to talk your way out of responsibility, that horrible nauseous feeling you get when the thought that she might be pregnant crosses your mind is there because you know the moral shit will hit you hardest. Girls get the babies, boys get the guilt. Girls who get pregnant are automatically going to get most of the sympathy, no matter how badly they behaved, and how properly you behaved. There's something about that bulge which makes

Sex tip no. 23: Condoms

They say that condoms can be gently worked into sexual foreplay. The idea is that you play around a bit with your penis exposed and then for the final bout of petting the girl slips it on for you. It's supposed to be arousing and teasing.

Is it?

Well, maybe, but it never seems appropriate, and it's rarely practical. First, it's extremely difficult to put a condom on a penis properly from the front. It's much easier when you're looking at it from behind like the penis's owner.

It gets all caught up in the pubic hair, all sorts of kinks and wrinkles get folded in, and sharp nails go through the rubber like semen through an IUD.

As for arousal, by the time you're both ready for the condom to be on, neither of you really gives a damn about foreplay.

Business is called for. Serious business. Teasing, amateurish, lingering, condom-application goes out of the window. The man takes over and just slaps it on as fast as he can.

---

normally right-thinking people go weak at the ethical knees.

So, you've got to protect your own corner. Only your mum will believe you when it comes out in the wash. Carry a packet of sheaths, nag your partner to get a new diaphragm if the old one's getting rather weary-looking, check she's still taking the Pill. The old fear used to be 'how on earth can you ask a girl if she's on the Pill or not'. The new one is whether you should believe her. With the Pill there's really not a lot you can do. The really cautious won't do anything without a sheath until they've managed to have a chat with the girl in which they discreetly get their views on accidental pregnancy across.

This is difficult because having persuaded a girl to get to home base you don't then want to give her a grilling about how safe and clean she is. If possible, on a date that seems to be going well early on, bring up the subject of pregnancies, children, and particularly abortion. Be tactful here. 'I've never fancied an abortion myself, how about you?' is not a good way of doing it. But if it transpires that you have a mid to late twenties or older lapsed Catholic who still believes vehemently that abortion is terrible and yet seems willing to go to bed with you, BE CAREFUL. Take your sheaths.

Danger signals need to be picked up early

MALE: Oh, no, I don't want kids until I'm at least forty-five. I'm just not old enough yet. And I know many couples who were getting along so well until she got pregnant, quite by accident. It just made everything go wrong.
GIRL: Oh.
MALE: And it's so unfair on the kid.

This conversation is going extremely well. Now comes the problem,

MALE: No, I really wouldn't want a child now.
FEMALE: Oh, come on, you'd feel different if you had one.

Those ten words should set alarms and red lights off all over your head. As things progress, be very cautious. If a diaphragm is being used or at least you're being told it's being used, you can check that it actually is in the course of foreplay. Don't lunge in and feel around, looking intently past your partner, concentrating every effort on deciding whether the ridges and lumps you're touching are rubber contraceptive parts, or the mysterious vaginal landscape. This is too obvious. You need to keep kissing, keep cuddling, and do it all gently, coincidentally.

If she says she's on the Pill you're going to have to trust

Sex tip no. 24: Buying Contraceptives

Buying contraceptives is traditionally the most embarrassing teenage skill that the heterosexual male has to master. Walking up to those ever-so-exposed counters, always staffed by women with white aprons, pulled back hair, and slightly scolding faces (or else by teenage shop girls who probably know your sister) and having to hold up a packet of Nu-Form or 'ribbed for extra fun' and hope that she serves you fast before anybody else sees you. This is an embarrassing purchase to make. It's screaming out, 'I'm hoping to be fucking tonight', and although the stereotyped male is macho, bestial, and doesn't give a damn, the majority of actual males are bundles of crawling sensitivity who like to keep the whole thing as discreet as possible.

There are one or two very simple things you can do to alleviate the really major embarrassment. First, don't walk up to the counter when there is a queue, this holds you up and makes your turn in the limelight clutching the condoms too long to be comfortable.

Never shop on a Saturday. That's when the teenage sales assistants are working. There's something about buying a contraceptive from someone you wouldn't mind using it with that's terribly unnerving. Don't despise the old system of making a string of purchases, but don't make contraceptives the last item. This gives the game away too fast. Make the rubbers the second to last item, and then ask a question about the last item, eg.,

MALE: A bottle of vitamin pills, some TCP, a 3-pack of Nu-Form, and have you got any of those cotton wool buds for ears, the extra thin ones?

This deflects attention from the sex-related purchase and gives your request an air of mundane normality.

If you still find it incredibly difficult you should practise buying other embarrassing items like tampons or eye make-up. And also bear in mind that things could have been a lot worse. A few years ago the contraceptive manufacturers were considering a plan to sell condoms in three sizes – small, medium and large.

---

her. If you really are suspicious, and yet so consumed with desire that you know you aren't going to be able to walk away without having had sex, there is a line of argument which usually gets you comfortably into a sheath-wearing position without undue embarrassment. Say that you're so excited that unless you put on a sheath (or two) to cut down the feeling, you're going to come too soon.

What to do if it bursts

Scares are just a fact of life. If you have sex you'll have scares. If you pull out at the end with strips of sheath hanging forlornly off your penis, you're obviously going to have to start worrying. Waves of regret and disbelief sweep over you followed by recrimination.

'I don't believe it, oh no, I don't believe it'. (*Disbelief.*)

'I'm never having sex again, my whole life is ruined, how can I go on, what's going to happen?'

This is then followed by anger, turning into self-pity.

Sex tip no. 25: High-risk Sheaths

One word of warning, when making love from behind, sheaths have the protective reliabilty of a paper bag. Stick to straightforward head-on-intercourse, or pile a few extra ones on. Also, always check the sell-by date on the packet you're using if you don't remember buying it. Sheaths actually have a pretty good shelf-life compared to soup and yoghurt but the results are a lot worse if they've gone off.

'The bastards who make these rotten sheaths should be made to pay for their mistakes, it's so unfair, it's so unfair. . . .

and then a final sinking into depression and gloom.

'She won't have an abortion, I'll be expected to marry her, a kid, a wife, oh god. I wonder how much air tickets to Rio cost?'

The stupid thing is that you don't even know if she's pregnant yet. It's hard to be cool about these scares, but it's only making it worse on yourself if you don't. Certainly you need to show that you don't share her pleasure. Hopefully you'll already have had an abortion/accidental pregnancy talk so that you can just give a quick recap here to refresh her memory. Then you need to remind her to look out for her next period, and keep asking her about it. Stay on the ball so that if you have to move early you can. But don't let it dominate your whole life.

Contraceptive Failure

So what's the story if the worst really comes to the worst? The period doesn't come, the morning sickness does. The pregnancy test confirms it. You say you're really not ready, she says she wants it.

Okay, now at this point it's time to start moving towards the bathroom for a long session of recrimination and tears. Now you're in trouble.

The problem for the non-macho male is that he is trapped in a moral loophole, 'the pregnancy trap'.

Let's look at how macho man and wimp man handle it.

First, the Wimp Man:

FEMALE: John, I went to the surgery this morning, and, well, we've got something to talk about.
WIMP MAN (*weakly*): Oh.

FEMALE: I'm pregnant.
WIMP MAN (*nauseous*): Oh god.

As the pressure piles up he tries a gambit which is the contraceptive equivalent of Sexspeak. He tries to appear to be a regular guy, but at the same time apply a little emotional blackmail.

WIMP MAN: Well, you know I'm not quite ready but you also know I feel the choice has to be yours. Whatever you decide I'll support you. It's your body and it's you who should make the choices.
FEMALE (*beaming*): Oh, I knew you'd be wonderful (*she hugs him*). Shall I call mother to tell her the good news?

The gambit was simple. Put the ball so completely in her court, act like a perfect New Man, and she'll actually be so overwhelmed that she gives in and lets him decide. No room for excuses, that's the wimp's ploy. Now it's cowardly, and it's high risk, but under this sort of pressure, it's completely understandable. It also fucked up completely.

Let's have a look at Macho Man getting the same news:

FEMALE: I went to the surgery today, and, well, there's something very important we need to talk about. I'm pregnant.
MACHO MAN: Is that right? Well you know I don't want a kid. What do you want to do?
FEMALE: Oh, well, I thought we might talk about it a bit, you know, go over the options.
MACHO MAN: Listen. You want the kid. Bye bye. You don't want the kid, I'll discuss options.

Now this sounds horrible, it's unenlightened, it's medieval, it's an indefensible position at any dinner party where less than half the guests are subscribers to *The Spectator*. But it does have a basic, moral justifiability. If it came down to a clean, calm discussion in front of an impartial judge, Macho Man, provided he stayed consistent, would be on fairly safe ground. It is the woman's body, so finally it

Sex tip no. 26: The G Spot

A bit like multiple orgasm for men, the G spot arrived with a great blast of publicity and then just disappeared completely. The fact is it's a bit of a joke.

The Sexual Reform Group, a San Francisco based collection of right-wing sexual activists have offered a $1000 reward for any man who can successfully find the G spots on five consecutive women. The fact that only nine men have even applied gives you some idea of the spot's stature.

In fact the whole idea of the world's male population, which can only hit the clitoris with about a 30 per cent strike rate, being able to find something as elusive as a G spot, buried deep inside, unknown even by the females themselves until *Cosmopolitan* came to the rescue, is quite laughable.

Don't worry about it.

---

must be her choice. If the man does want it, and she doesn't, he must accept it and go Dutch on the abortion. If the woman does want it and the man doesn't, but she agrees to go with him, he must again go Dutch. But if the woman does want it, and the man doesn't, and she decides to go through with it, should he have to support her decision for the rest of his life?

Obviously, if he's made it clear all along that he doesn't want a child, he is under no such moral imperative. Macho Man knows this, just says 'fuck it', and leaves. Wimp Man vacillates, either gives in, or does a runner in the night.

But then the pressure is enormous. Do the runner, however brazenly or self-confidently, and it is tough. At the very best you'll be the villain of the piece. At the worst you'll look like Attila the Hun.

It's a hard life. Bite the bullet, or choke on it.

Women and Durex

There is one additional happenstance which you need to be prepared for. In these liberated days, it has been known for more experienced women to pack their own Durex. This is really very sensible, but can strike the unprepared male as a little intimidating. IT ACTUALLY MEANS SHE'S BEEN THINKING THE SAME THOUGHTS AS HE HAS. This is frightening. Men feel a little safer when they think women don't know that they're thinking. The moment they think they do, and even worse, that they're way ahead, it's a little unsettling. The key here is to smile and go 'Hey, yeah, great, huh' for as long as it takes for you to get your breath back. Don't be surprised.

Orgasms

Post-climactic trauma ('spermicidal blues')

It's a contrast every bit as great as the opening contrast of fantasies that began the book. The moment a male and female have climaxed, having been roughly on the same sensory road up till then (similar noises, similar bucking movements, etc.) they are suddenly flung apart in completely different directions. Girls can get terribly emotional, even the most passionate and apparently physical of girls can want you to become very tender, to give them a hug, to stroke their hair, that sort of thing. The man, unfortunately, just isn't there at all. As the warm glow of release about the groin fades, he goes off everything, sex, intimacy, warmth, affection, the works. All he wants to do is roll over and forget all about it.

GIRL: Oh, ahh, ohh, ahh, aaah.
MAN: Aah, oohh, ohh, ahha.
(They both come.)
GIRL: Oh, Geoff, hug me, that was so nice, please hold me.

MAN (*grunts and begins to hug absent-mindedly*). Did I post the mortgage cheque? I hope I paid in those expenses, shit, I forgot the milk, you'd think she might have remembered. She still owes me that £5. . . .

It's really bad practice to do this, and it's biting the hand that feeds you. Force yourself to hug her, you'll both be asleep very fast.

Sex tip no. 27: Premature Ejaculation

This really isn't too much of a problem, it's an embarrassment of riches, if you like, which is infinitely better than an inability to make anything stir down there. If you haven't had sex for a while, really are being driven wild by a particular girl, or are in the relatively early stages of sexual exploration, there is always a danger that your excitement is going to come to a head too soon. It is, however, easily controlled. If you think you can hang on long enough to get to the bedroom and the really serious sex, two or three sheaths pulled on one on top of the other will normally so deaden the feeling that you'll be able to hang on for a respectable amount of time. If you're a little anxious that it's all going to happen a lot earlier, the answer is a bout of masturbation before the date begins. Some lovers will use this technique just before going to bed with their partners, but the drawback of this is the moment you've come, you tend to go completely off sex and feel a little sleepy. With your girlfriend lying in bed, tingling in the glow of sexual expectation, you just want to bring the TV in and doze off in front of the late show. But by masturbating at seven o'clock before an eight o'clock date, with probably no heavy petting till about eleven o'clock, everything is kept under control, without all interest being stamped out.

If you don't climax together

This whole business of climaxing is really too confusing to worry about too much. When a man climaxes it's so obvious, there can be no question about whether he did or not, whether it was faked, all that stuff. It happens, bang, and suddenly there are yoghurt stains all over the place. Women, on the other hand, are far more complex. They can have multiple orgasms, different types of orgasms, enjoy sex and still have no orgasm at all. It's really confusing. It's actually very hard to tell when they have had an orgasm at all.

If you're helping a girlfriend of yours along to an orgasm with your finger, it's very difficult to know when to stop. She'll groan louder and quieter, shuffle and move about, but not in any sequential fashion, just in waves as they come and go. The thing to do is just to keep on until you get some instruction to do something different.

Problems occur if at the end of the serious sex, she hasn't had an orgasm yet. If you sense this you're left with a moral obligation to finish her off. You can't just roll over and fall asleep, no matter how much you want to. You're probably going to have to ask to establish if she really hasn't had it. This is okay, it makes you look sensitive and considerate, but you have to do it in the right way.

Wrong

MALE: Ahhhhhhhhh. (*He comes.*)

FEMALE: MmmmmmmmmmH, ahhhh, ohhhh. . . . (*She doesn't come.*)

MALE (*slumping onto the bed, rubbing his eyes*). God, I'm exhausted. (*Looks over.*) Are you finished yet?

This isn't a very sensitively asked question, you'd need to be Germaine Greer to answer yes to this one. So how should you ask?

Right

MALE: Ahhhhhhhh. (*He comes.*)
FEMALE: Oh, oh, ah, ah, oh. . . . (*She doesn't come.*)
MALE (*hugging girl tightly*): Shall I help you with my finger?

This question is so sweetly asked, and so affectionately put that you might even get away with not having to do anything at all. It could just become a hug and a doze-off situation.

If it doesn't, if the girl says, 'that would be nice', you can go to it safe in the knowledge that you're investing in your future sex life. The chief danger is that your weariness and completely turned off libido will let you fall asleep while you're working on your partner. This is a terrible thing to do, and virtually writes off the whole thing. You MUST stay awake during the fingering process. This actually isn't easy.

You really don't get a lot of feedback from the clitoris, and you can never tell how much longer you're going to have to wait.

The best way of combating the fatigue is to concentrate all your remaining energy on what's happening underneath your middle finger. Explore the area, push the little nomad from side to side, try and find where he goes, a sort of clitoral hide and seek. The more interested you become, the less likelihood there will be of dozing off, and probably the faster the girl will come.

Sex in the morning

You know how horrible you can feel in the morning. Your breath can strip paint at 150 yards, your teeth bulge with plaque, your body is as stiff as your most virulent erection. The last thing in the world you could ever imagine wanting is sex.

DON'T BELIEVE IT.

Morning sex is very often the most stupendous sex you'll ever have. The thing about it is that it has to be started

Sex tip no. 28: Intercourse

While making love there are some common, slightly embarrassing things which it is better to think about before, than panic over during. First is knowing what to do with your eyes. The problem that we had with kissing is even more extreme when you're actually having intercourse. Men do tend to like seeing what's going on. Girls tend to lie back, shut their eyes, and enjoy it. The problem arises when you suddenly find yourself staring straight into her eyes. Whatever happens you've got to look warm and affectionate. You can't just look away at whatever bit of the action is interesting you. You need to look involved, concerned, and sensitive, not concentrating hard and in the throws of callous passion. If you can't make yourself look warm, go for the hug and a brief break.

---

slowly and then performed carefully. There probably won't be a lot of kissing because neither of you will smell or taste very nice.

However if you just start hugging, and then stroking a little, you should find that those morning stretches get mixed in with EMH stretches, and in no time at all you're positively raring to go.

CHAPTER 7

Oral Sex

In a massive survey of American prostitutes last year it was discovered that over 75 per cent of customers didn't want the kinks, the S and M, the pelting with fresh cream cakes. They wanted straight oral sex. As one leading professional put it 'if more women in America got down on their knees more often, we'd be out of business'.

The fact is that oral sex is one of the nicest ways a man can come. Despite all its symbolic significance, its link with childbirth and the womb, all that stuff, vaginas just don't do to penises what mouths can. That isn't to dismiss vaginas but it is to put them in their proper place – on a level with the mouth.

Nobody's quite sure where the idea for oral sex first came from. It seems pretty improbable when you think about it, and this is probably one of its fascinations for men. Men look at their penises, obviously with affection, but also with a sense of disbelief. They can't believe that something that ugly could ever be desirable to a girl. The idea of someone being willing to put it in her mouth is quite extraordinary.

Now, some girls may in fact share this male sense of disbelief that anyone should want to suck it, but many other, really very intelligent, entirely balanced, very polite and pleasant girls do not. They have no qualms about it.

They are willing to suck a penis.

Those words should be left to resonate because they are so thrilling.

The problem is getting to the point, etiquette-wise, where a girl who is willing to do it feels able to do it without appearing too forward.

Because of the male sense of incredulity, girls naturally feel a little odd performing fellatio for the first time. They don't want to be thought dirty or too easy. So it's the man's job to make it as easy as possible.

MAN: I'll give you £50 if you go down on me.

This won't work.

Equally ineffective is the ploy which tries to introduce oral sex into conversation as a joke in the hope that the girl will take the hint. This sounds like a good idea especially if you've been getting off with a girl for a while, maybe even sleeping with her, and she hasn't made any moves in that direction yet.

But the problem is that if you start to tell oral sex jokes, make little references to it, all that sort of stuff, it's a bit like shoving a girl's hand onto your penis in the car during petting. She suddenly becomes self-conscious, aware of herself, feels awkward for not having done it before, and too observed doing it now. A block builds up and you're left to dream about what it would be like.

No, the right way to suggest it is with your body. Just the same technique that you used in the car with your penis rubbing on her thigh. Suggest physically, not verbally.

Now the verb 'suggest' is used specifically for a reason. 'Suggest' does not mean, 'grab her head and shove it between your thighs', nor does it mean, 'plead and beg'. As you thrash around try and roll your penis about as many bits of her body as possible, and gradually manoeuvre it into a position where it's within striking distance of her mouth. Then let her decide about taking the plunge.

Once the plunge has been taken you can't afford to lie back and enjoy it completely. You've got to remember to resist the overwhelming desire to start holding her head firmly down on your groin (this can be a little disconcerting and lead to severe choking), and you've also got to watch

Sex tip no. 29: S and M

For most people the whole business of actually finding someone to have sex with involves quite enough S and M to be going along with. Others cry out for studs and leather and screams.

So what points can a novice S and M enthusiast take in to the torture chamber?

1. Always have talcum powder shaken on the inside of any rubber bondage clothing. It makes it so much easier to get out of afterwards.
2. Make your whips out of string, not rope. It saves the carpet from blood stains.
3. In the event of blood stains salt works brilliantly.
4. Only use granny knots or double granny knots for bondage games.
5. Nipple clamps should not be customized from old bulldog clips, they are much too highly sprung.
6. The S and M video is a *A Woman in Flames* in German with sub-titles.
7. Sterilize all stilettoes at the start.
8. Keep leather crops and boots well buffed with saddle polish to make them as squeaky as possible.

---

out for teeth. Be ready to adjust a little in case you start getting grazed.

To start off with, don't move your hips too much. Let her do all the moving so that she is completely in control. Only when you're both a little more used to it can you politely start to buck up and down. This can be a little frustrating to start off with, but it is good manners.

Girls with fringes can be a little frustrating. Again, because of the basic sense of incredulity that anyone could be willing to do this to a penis, you'll notice a desire to watch what's going on. The sight is definitely worth a look, even if it's only snatched. The problem is that fringes, and long hair in general, curtain everything. You can bend your upper body round to one side and catch a glimpse, but this does rather draw attention to yourself and you'll suddenly find your partner looking back at you as she performs which would be really exciting if it wasn't so embarrassing. You don't know whether to smile and then look away, or just look back and wave, ('oh, hi, huh, fancy seeing you').

As your climax approaches decisions have to be made fast. Are you going to come in her mouth, has this been agreed? Will you be able to make love to her afterwards? On later blow-jobs you can leave this decision-making up to her, but on early ones you need to decide and be as gentle as possible. If nothing has been said at all, it's better not to finish in her mouth. If she really wasn't expecting it the shock could mean 'never again'.

If you are allowed to come in her mouth it's as well to understand just how difficult a procedure this can be. The problem isn't the coming, it's the hypersensitivity that follows it. You see the girl can't always tell when you start to come, and sometimes she will continue to pound away good-naturedly right through those first bursts. This is incredibly uncomfortable – it feels as if you've got five bladders and they're all about to explode simultaneously. So as you're about to come you need to hug her, hold her, or do something to let her know she must stay still for a moment.

Doing Oral Sex On a Girl

Fellatio and cunnilingus are always being confused. Sloanes remember which are which by nicknaming fellatio 'Freddie', and cunnilingus 'Caroline', the name indicating the sex which is lying back and enjoying it. Now cunnilingus, or as it is sometimes known in *Forum* 'worshipping at the altar of Venus', is really not a particularly big deal. It's overlaid with all sorts of mysterious technical and spiritual jargon, when in fact what it all comes down to is Scout's Honour with your tongue.

'If little girls are made of sugar and spice and all things nice', observed one of history's great experimental lovers, 'why do they taste of anchovies?' This is true, girls do tend to taste of anchovies, but it is rarely the overpowering, tastebud-searing blast which some men fear. Also, as long as you confine your attention to the nomadic clitoris in the upper, surface reaches of the area, you avoid a lot of the richer stuff lower down, and further in. The real drawback is the pubic hair, which gets stuck in your teeth, and also neck and tongue strain. After about thirty seconds your tongue really gets stiff.

After a minute your neck follows suit. But it's acceptable to call up reinforcements from your fingers while you rest your head for a few minutes if the orgasm is taking a while to come. Once it's all over you're left with a mouthful of slightly fishy saliva, and the odd hair. It really isn't that hard swallowing and there's never actually that much as long as you've kept dribbling throughout the proceedings. Try not to spit too obviously if you decide against the swallow. This is rude.

CHAPTER 8

Periods

Everything the average man needs to know about periods: If it doesn't come you start to worry.

SCENE: SUBURBAN HOME, DAY
(*A kitchen laid for breakfast. The family enter.*)
FATHER: Pass the marmalade, son.
SON: Sure, dad.
MOTHER: So, Susan, how did you find the bleeding this morning? Lighter or still pretty heavy?
SUSAN: Well, sort of. . . .
SON: Oh, give us a break, Mum, not over the eggs.
FATHER: Yes, let's save it, dear.
MOTHER: This is important, men shouldn't be excluded from these things. We're living in a different world now. Susan?
SUSAN: About the same.
MOTHER: Well, maybe you'd better take an ST just in case. What's an ST, son?
SON: A sanitary towel, mum.
MOTHER: And what's it for, dear?
FATHER: Well, for absorbing the er. . . . Oh look, this is ridiculous, I've had enough.
(*He leaves.*)
MOTHER: Luddite.
SUSAN: I think you mean revanchist.

Enlightened mothers try and encourage husbands and sons to share in the arrival of daughters at womanhood and sanitary towels. Discharge and PMT are discussed at breakfast over the polyunsaturates, men volunteering to do the shopping are asked to pick up Lil-lets and Tampax – family-size cartons (actually the most difficult thing for a man to buy – it makes buying contraceptives look laughably simple).

A lot of this is pretty hard to take. But the alert male realizes early on that there is a certain bravado attached to knowing all the ins and outs of the female cycle.

The menstrual cycle does tend to be a little frightening to men because it is so mysterious, and involves the use of strange equipment and weird rituals which can unnerve him. The result is it becomes endowed with all sorts of folklore and superstitions. Does PMT really exist? What are those curious pieces of string you catch glimpses of beneath her underwear? Why won't she take off her pants in bed? What happens if you have sex while it's all still going on?

Frankly, who knows? The best move here is to leave the whole thing in the girl's hands. If something crops up, and it's getting in the way, let her bring it up. You're always going to be an amateur in this field, so keep an amateur's attitude – occasional, good-natured interest.

If you're not reading this at breakfast take a look at the next section.

The Menstrual Cycle

How does it work?

The thing itself is pretty straightforward. Once a month the female body starts teeing up an egg for fertilization. After a few days it drives it off to the Fallopian tubes where it waits for a couple of *weeks* in the hope of some sperm fighting its way through and fertilizing it. If none makes the grade, then it passes away and the womb, which has been getting ready for pregnancy, sheds its lining.

It's the business of catching the falling lining which keeps Lil-lets and Tampax in the black.

Safe sex

Well, there's really no such thing. But roughly speaking the middle two weeks are the fertile ones when the egg might be sitting in the tubes with its finger on the trigger.

Can you do it during a period?

You certainly can, and according to Shere Hite many women love the idea of it. But really it all depends on the girl. If the period is on the heavy side the whole thing can get a bit messy and you're advised to bring along towels and a change of pyjamas, hot water and shampoo. If it's light, then you're just talking in terms of the odd stain which is really no problem. Manners insist, however, that if you start you don't stop at the last moment. You have to go through with it. Also, when you've finished you mustn't too obviously inspect your penis. Peep discreetly but steer clear of the,

MAN (*pulling out*): Oh Jesus, look at the colour of it!

This is difficult for a girl to accept.

What are those bits of string which you sometimes see hanging from her pants?

These are the rip cords of her tampons. You pull these to get the cotton wool plug out after its work is done. You'll sometimes notice them wrapped up in her handbag. They look a bit like toffee lollipops from the outside.

How can you tell when a girl's having a period?

Bad breath, spots, tears, wearing underpants in bed, doubling up with cramps, pressing herself against the fridge and going 'ahhhh', cutting up your clothes with a bread knife when you ask for the salt, and, most of all, clumsiness are all symptoms of the condition.

What do you do when a girl is having a period?

Avoid confrontation, let her take the lead. Be malleable and quiche-eating. Boldness and machismo don't go with menstruation.

CHAPTER 9

Erections

Erections really are curious beasts. Most of the time they are very predictable, they respond to the same sexual clichés time after time (hence the success of the dirty magazine market). This does make potentially erection-inspiring events fairly easy to predict and plan for. And they must be planned for. Erections, unlike suntans or muscles, are not physical features which are acceptable to go swinging around in public. People on the whole are embarrassed by them, none more so than their owners. Few men haven't at some time or another cupped their latest erection in their hand and given it a careful inspection, aghast at the fact that anyone, particularly a girl, could find such a strange-looking thing attractive. They look like the sort of thing you should be embarrassed about having in your pocket, and every man knows it and feels it. If God had wanted us to be proud of them, he'd have made them better looking, goes the logic.

Their nature is also misunderstood.

Certain bestsellers (*Man's Best Friend*) would have us believe that erections are benevolent troublemakers, any no good they get up to, they generally get up to by trying to get up women.

In fact the erection feels no great bond of loyalty to its owner. They are linked by pure chance. We think we use them, have fun with them. The reverse is true. Erections are in fact a thinking, breathing breed apart. And when they call the tune only the most strong-minded of men can refuse to dance.

Everyone's got that terrible fear of having an erection in a public place. There's one part of us that still feels sex is dirty, which makes thoughts about sex dirty, and whereas girls just get a little damp and a touch of stiffness about the nipples (entirely invisible apart from swimwear calendar pictures), men get a throbbing, tumescent mass bursting from their groins at the slightest murmur of an erotic afterthought. Despite sexual equality, despite *Playgirl*, despite permissiveness, despite the fact that it's a bigger lie than 'cheque's in the mail', 'I won't come in your mouth', girls are still thought to have fewer dirty thoughts than men. They have somehow managed to corner the market in lying back and thinking of England (possibly because getting on top and thinking of England is a less effective metaphor). They are the ones who have things done to them, the victims, not the aggressors. But in fact the truth is they just hide it better.

The terrible thing about erections is that they are as attracted to trouble as they are to sex. Take that most recurrent of male nightmares of tumescent discovery – the men's changing room erection. You're standing there in the corner, getting undressed, quite innocently, with really nothing on your mind, and you suddenly become aware that you've been looking at other men's penises. You're not looking out of any sexual interest, you're not even looking because you want to compare yours to theirs. You're just looking, without even noticing it, absent-mindedly. Somehow, the synapse that fires the thought in your brain, 'I'm looking at other men's penises, fires so loudly it rouses the sleeping erection from its cave inside your groin. Nothing happens at first, but you know it's awake and watching. It just hasn't got up yet. You suddenly realize that if any of the other men in the changing room have been watching you watching them, they might think that you're homosexual. You start looking hard at their faces (never lower), hard at locker doors, hard at the tiles

Sex tip no. 30: Underwear

Really a very surprisingly large number of girls do on occasions wear underwear which men would describe as 'sexy' or 'dirty'.

The reasons behind man's undying fascination for suspender belts, stockings, and suspenders are so deeply embedded now that it is really very difficult to work out. The power of these strange garments seem Jungian in its ability to transcend cultures and countries. One Brazilian male, interviewed in the course of this book, admitted that he had never seen stockings and suspenders. All the girls in his country, he pointed out, wore nothing or very little underneath. When he was shown a picture of a woman wearing them he was converted immediately and promptly ordered two sets to take back to Rio. There is nothing quite as wonderful as that moment when your hand is sliding up a girl's leg on what you assume is a pair of tights, and it suddenly slides onto a ring of skin about the thigh. It supercharges everything.

Women understand the power of these instruments of suspension and support. They enjoy wearing them too, and if they already do it on their own it's not generally too hard to persuade them to wear them occasionally in bed.

Girls who don't wear them, ever, are more difficult. Or at least seem more difficult.

Men tend to feel that they will be slapped and accused of degeneracy if they were to suggest buying a pair to fool around in. And yet, if asked, a surprising number of non-wearers are quite happy to give it a go. The thing about them is that unlike the more bizarre forms of dressing up (French maids, rubber, etc.), stockings and suspenders do have a practical daily application, are something which their mothers wore, and can even be bought in Marks & Spencers and C & A's. There's a very safe surface to them. Because of this often the best way of bringing the subject up is to buy a pair while you're out shopping together. Make a bit of a joke of it. You'll have her won over in no time.

---

directly below your feet. All in an attempt to look as unhomosexual as possible.

The result?

You start to look exactly like a homosexual trying not to be noticed in the changing rooms. As this fear works its way into your erection's cave, your erection, still dormant, begins to raise its head and sniff the trouble. It starts to swell with your fears of being thought gay. Unless you act fast you're going to have a full-scale erection on your hands in a matter of seconds.

The answer?

You have to talk it down.

This is a highly complicated technique, every bit as tough as the more widely known versions used to bring unpiloted aircraft safely to the ground. The key is concentration. To be successful you have to catch the erection early. It's the first tremors of excitement that are the weakest, the first fifteen seconds of tumescence are the erection's Achilles heel, and this is where the concerned owner must strike. Once it's fully upright and cantilevering itself into position, the growing friction with your underwear and trousers keeps exciting it more and you may as well start introducing it to anyone standing nearby because it's so visible it's virtually shaking hands.

Traditional talking down technique involves immediately throwing your mind into some intellectual game, so dry and so distant that all thoughts of sex are driven away. Pythagoras's theorem, the alphabet in reverse, the thirteen times table are all much tried favourites. But the fact is that while some admirably strong-willed owners can pull this method off under the most terrible pressure, the majority cannot. That's one of the tricky things about erections. They start off by looking at something they like, or hearing something they like, but the moment they've

Sex tip no. 31: How to Tell When You're Randy

Some mornings you will wake up to find your hormones working overtime. The EMH that stirred lazily first thing stays stiff for hours; you will start looking for that old dirty magazine you kept up in the cupboard, and when you find it keep turning repeatedly to the ads for porno videos, dirty letters, and massage services. You might even try dialling the numbers a few times. On public transport and in the street you will scrutinize the top of every woman's skirt trying to discover if she's wearing stockings and suspenders by those tell-tale bumps and curves. The Pretty Polly underwear ads on the Tube will seem powerfully erotic, you'll start looking at dirty film times in the evening papers, every woman you talk to you'll lose concentration and wonder if she ever does oral sex. This state is called 'being randy'.

---

started they start making up their own fantasies to speed everything up.

SCENE: A COCKTAIL PARTY, NIGHT

Groups of sleekly attired women stand around dinner-jacketed men. Charles has just been introduced to Vicki who, as she talks, takes the olive from her Martini and starts to suck it. An erection stirs.

CHARLES (*to himself*): 13 × 13 is 49, 13 × 4 is 52, 13 × 5 is . . . .

ERECTION (*over*): Her lips closed around the olive, sucking it slowly, firmly as her fingers ran down the side of my face.

CHARLES (*more intently*): 13 × 6 is 72, 13 × 8 is 104 . . . .

ERECTION: She rested her hands on my lips and began to slide her satiny thighs slowly across the front of my trousers, still looking at me, her mouth slightly open, the olive resting on her tongue.

By this time the game is, frankly, over. The line of Charles's dress is becoming strangely contorted around the hips, and any moment now Vicki is going to spot it. So Charles has to hurriedly excuse himself and rush off to another part of the room where he probably won't dare talk to her, or anyone she talks to, for the rest of the evening, just in case she saw.

So what can be done? A far more effective method of combatting an insistent erection is the Zen approach to the talk down. Rather than trying to get the erection off your mind, you fill your mind with it, with exactly how it feels as it grows larger, which bits go hard first, how fast it's rising, everything. By concentrating on how it feels, something far more tangible and easier to grasp than Pythagoras or the alphabet, you stamp out the erotic thoughts and often nip it in the bud.

There is also the Clint Eastwood method, a variant of the Zen technique with a slight Hollywood cachet, but because it involves prolonged eye contact with the offending erection it has to be kept for unwanted erections in the privacy of your own home. It consists, literally, of staring right at your erection, daring it to keep on rising. 'Make my day, punk', you need to say to it. Study it closely, laugh at its ungainly appearance, those strange veins running down the side, the ridiculous cluster of wiry pubic hair. Shame it into flaccidity. This can work wonders.

EMH Erections

There are certain times when erections can be particularly troublesome, and also very hard to explain. EMH is the most common of these. EMH, (or early morning hardness), is that totally asexual erection that you often find peeping out of your pyjama trousers when you first wake up in the morning. These can often get you in serious trouble because if you happen to have a girl with you they will naturally feel flattered and will frequently turn amorous in return when sex is actually the last thing you were thinking of. The annoying thing about EMH is that it can occur at almost any time of the day or night, usually when you're feeling a little tired, and generally has nothing to do with being excited. EMH is unfortunately highly resistant to 'talk down' techniques. You have to resort to the hand in the pocket, the bag held across the groin, or just have a long lie-in.

That other form of supremely inconvenient erection is the erection you get when you really want to go to the lavatory. This is, according to reliable sources within the Church, one of the punishments that traditionally has to be endured by those waiting in purgatory for a final decision on their future arrangements. It is the most frustrating condition, again entirely unrelated to sex, but often as hard and throbbing as any that you're ever likely to get. The immediate need here is generally less for disguise, and more for a way of getting the erection down far enough to allow you to go to the lavatory. No woman could ever grasp the degree of frustration that such erections cause. But imagine standing before a lavatory bowl, with the lid up and bladder full, with an erection pointing directly at the ceiling. Generally what the owner will try and do is bend it down as far as it will go and then try and lean over sideways, firing it across his hip. The particular problem with getting this type of erection down is that although they respond well to the Zen technique they also tend to spring back up again every time the bladder flexes. If you really get in trouble it's just a matter of gritting your teeth and bending it.

Men's Underwear

It's because fashionable recently for men to start switching to boxer shorts from the more traditional Y-front design. Don't sneer. Underwear selection is important, especially if you hope to be in an undressed situation with a girl later on in the evening. So when you think there's a chance of getting to that stage don't slip into the indelibly stained, orange acrylic pants your mother gave you when you were fourteen which have somehow withstood the stretches of time. Go for something simpler, less synthetic, less tight. Doctors don't like tight underpants, they say it kills sperm and induces impotence. Girl-hungry men should avoid them for the simple reason that a tight pair of pants tends to force erections into curious, twisted shapes which become excruciatingly painful and won't respond to the more deft, discreet touches through your trousers pockets due to the tautness of the fabric. Some unfortunate sufferers have described the embarrassment caused by the rapid, radical adjustments that the pain makes imperative as so intense they actually come away sunburnt. Learn the lesson, keep your underwear loose.

Coming back to the boxer shorts/Y-fronts dilemma, boxer shorts can look a little bulky in some pairs of trousers, but their inherent looseness is a good thing. And they do avoid the strange slit in the front of the trad Y-front design which archaeologists believe was originally intended for the penis to be threaded through for urinating. As anyone who has tried this will tell you, it's an awkward job, often requiring your penis to be wrenched up and slightly to the side. Having contorted it into this position, with its head squashed sideways out through the opening, and the elastic in your pants throttling it, you are supposed to urinate. In fact it's quite impossible. What's really funny is that it's supposed to save you time by allowing you to forget about unzipping your trousers.

The result is you're left with that terrible feeling of guilt as you stand at the urinal with nothing happening while the stalls on either side change several times. And as everyone in public lavatories is too embarrassed to look at their own relief operations and therefore watches other people's you know they're wondering what the fuck you're doing down here, and that you're probably a bender trying to watch other men's willies. Anyway it's a ghastly invention. But quite apart from that, its real problem for the sexually active male is that erections, being basically mischievous creatures, always seem to find a way of poking their heads through this ridiculous opening, making it almost impossible to tuck back in discreetly.

Eventually you have to pull the pant material, and your erection, out at a right angle and then loop it over the end of the penis. Try and buy pants with the hole on the opposite side to your normal erection growth. Or stick with boxers.

Urinating and Orgasms

If you're about to have sex with someone, and have your erection ready, but also need to go to the lavatory, don't be tempted not to go. It's worth the wait and the frustration because when orgasms compete with the bladder it's never as much fun. You're left with a problem, however, namely, explaining the delay to your partner. She is raring to go, your erection is raring to go, and yet you insist on rushing off to the bathroom where you proceed to sit and chat to her through the door for fifteen minutes or so. Of course you can never tell her the truth unless you're both getting on incredibly well, or have been going out for some time. Even then it's best to stay away from too much lavatory sharing. One quite good excuse is that you always like to wash thoroughly before sex. This has a good, nutritional, fresh-faced, polyunsaturate feel to it, and is in everyone's vested interest. Of course with this line though it's important not to stay too long or else the girl will begin to assume that you must have been absolutely filthy dirty to start with, and will probably be a little less enthusiastic.

CHAPTER 10

When the Fantasy Bites Back

It's typical of the heterosexual male that the thing he dreams of most is also the thing that frightens him the most: being picked up by a beautiful girl. It happens to everyone at least once in their lives, and it is the ultimate test of sexual mettle.

Okay, you're sitting by a pool in the middle of somewhere tropical. It's lined with oiled bodies, screaming kids, and cheap ghetto blasters. Lying here in your corner you can watch the available female talent in their high-hipped one-pieces and fronded bikinis (Brazilian style is all the rage this year).

Your mirrored sunglasses let you look without being seen. It's almost like a dirty magazine, except the girls are all real, and moving. You lie there fantasizing.

FANTASY 1: One girl plunges into the pool, swims with lazy athleticism over to your side of the pool, then pulls herself out in front of you. She pulls her hair back then comes forward and starts rubbing oil into your shoulders, into your stomach, into your legs. She drops her room key into your lap, rests her left hand momentarily on your thigh, then walks away towards the hotel.

This is the standard set-up. Lone male as sexual hunter, taking up his position away in the corner, watching, waiting. It's like a dirty magazine sort of feeling. Playing out secret fantasies.

You've been here twenty minutes now and the girls aren't showing any obvious interest in you. It's a little annoying but you can handle it. You just lie back and fantasize some more.

FANTASY 2: You pick up her room key and walk to the mysterious girl's room, enter, and find that she's showering. You join her. You take her. Under the streams of water.

Everything remains standard. No girls are expressing any interest so the fantasies get a little more aggressive. It's all still pretty safe.

One of the girls over on your left has now been staring at you over the top of her sunglasses for the last thirteen minutes. She's got up and walked past twice, she's stretched out in front of you on the rim of the pool. Each time you take a peak at her she's still lying there, staring right back. You look away quickly. You want to go to the lavatory but that will mean walking past the place where she's lying and you know that she'll be looking at you the whole way. You're feeling very self-conscious. She's got an unbelievable body contained in a designer slashed one-piece. She keeps on looking at you over the top of her glasses. It's so arch, so contrived, so obvious. You don't dare look back. You cannot believe she means it. Maybe she's a hooker, you're sure this is the sort of thing they do to get clients. You keep looking around to see if there's anyone else standing nearby she could be looking at. There isn't. What do you do? You're dying to go to the lavatory. You're late for lunch. But you're transfixed by her stare.

This is the classic male reaction to a fantasy standing up and biting him in the neck. He is terrified. Learn this lesson: Sometimes it looks like girls are ignoring you so much that you must just be horrendous looking. In fact it's often the opposite. They could well like you but know that you're watching them, and just get nervous. To a man the idea of walking past a building-site full of women, their bottom halves showing through their ill-fitting jeans and vests, being whistled and heckled, is absolutely wonderful. The reality is terrifying.

Fortunately in these situations so much of the running is being made by the girl that as long as you don't deter her physically from continuing (asking how much she costs, giving her the finger, looking at her pointedly then turning to your side and pretending to throw up by shoving a finger down the back of your throat) she will continue. What you need is the courage of your libido. Look up and look straight back at her. She has made the first move, all you need to do is return the ball.

She will then tell you what to do. She'll most likely wave you over to her.

NEVER go. Smile and wave back. She'll then come over to you. Then you can start the conversation. But remember you're under no pressure here. She is making all the moves. You're playing the passive female part. This is an education. Learn from it. Obviously encourage her, but in the gaps in the conversation let her lead. Just look away and smile winsomely while you wait for her to say something else.

Coping with a Woman Who Becomes Violently Turned On

The funny thing about men is that though they are required to lead, and often kick against the duties that involves, they get terrified when the lead is taken away. An idle bathroom fantasy over a quick lunchtime wank is a safe way of dreaming of being dominated. But in the front seat of the car, or the back seat of the Penge Oden, it can be unnerving if your partner is transformed by your tentative kiss into a sexual cannibal, tearing at your clothes. On the verge of eating you alive. But, you see, the curious thing is that sexually, women tend to lose themselves far faster than men. Just think of it, the man has to go on top most of the time, has to pump his thighs, prop himself up on his arms, plot and orchestrate the seduction, lead and gauge the girl's response. He has to stay more conscious, so he retains a greater capacity for suddenly becoming embarrassed. Sexual performance is the ultimate status-giving skill. Under-perform, or make some terrible gaffe, and the male ego has to go into intensive care.

Girls, on the other hand, get into the sex far faster once the initial obstacles are removed. They let the males worry about the logistics, they just enjoy the feeling. When the feeling starts provoking their bodies they can respond very violently.

The key, if it frightens you, is to slow down the speed, the noise level, and the pressure of all contact. Go for a lot more stroking and nuzzling than panting and sucking. Make it more affectionate than passionate. This calms everything down, but keeps the libido straining just under the surface. You can then choose the perfect moment for its release at your leisure.

Other men just say surrender. (Ask a girl to kiss you like a male, sticking her tongue into your mouth – it feels strange at first but is actually quite nice after a while.) Once you've got over the shock and the disorientation of not leading, that is really quite nice too.

CHAPTER 11

Love in Planes

For some strange reason lost in the darkest recesses of the male libido, pressurized cabins cruising at 33,000 feet are among the most actively fantasized about sexual practice grounds known to the modern erection. In competition with air sickness bags, in-flight movies, and plastic containerized food, even stockings and suspenders, your best friend's girl and the French maid pale in sexual comparison.

But how efficient is the average plane cabin for the sexual encounter?

In physical terms it's not really that friendly an environment for erections. Your skin flakes, your feet and bladder swell, your mind is jet-lagged into a state of numbed lethargy. Yet one in four business travellers fantasizes about in-flight sexual encounters.

Why?

Well, you know that jet-lagged feeling. It's like a waking sleep. You can't get any real sleep, but you're too tired to stay awake. You're tired and bored and uncomfortable, with nothing to occupy you but the stewardesses walking up and down the aisle. This environment produces a sort of EMH feeling in your penis. It yawns, it stretches, it turns into an erection, and then the thoughts come. One of the stewardesses seems to be wearing a bra so tight that her nipples almost show through it. Is that blonde girl wearing a suspender belt? Is it just coincidence or is that brunette smiling at you a little too often?

If you're after sex in the plane, stewardesses aren't, however, the percentage shot. Most of the time they're worked off their feet, and by the point of the flight when the chores ease off, they've developed a healthy distaste for the public on board. You do hear stories of passengers being invited by stewardesses into the special room which is kept for them above the cargo bay just under first class, or into the lavatories, but this really is mostly the stuff of fantasy. Asking a stewardess out though, is a perfectly fair shot. Many of them find that they never get asked out enough because male passengers are always too intimidated, and are often delighted if you take the trouble. It's probably a good idea to use a note, or a discreet word late in the flight when she's in the kitchen, or near first class, so that you're away from rows of bored fellow passengers with nothing better to do than watch you make a fool of yourself in the event of your being shot down in flames. Remember to maintain face, and limit the damage by always keeping proposals as one-on-one as possible.

Come-ons from fellow passengers are a far more frequent occurrence. It must be the boredom and the desperate anonymity of economy class travel, but you will occasionally find yourself being looked back at long and hard by a woman sitting nearby.

In an aircraft you can really afford to throw a lot of caution to the wind. You're together for such a short period of time before being scattered all over the super-apex world the moment you land that there is really little danger of any massively embarrassing failures pursuing you home. If you detect an enthusiastic look, follow it up and see what happens.

Sex in the lavatory or on the seat?

Sexual tradition as imbibed by generations of masturbating teenagers from the *Emmanuelle* films has it that airline sex takes place largely in the lavatories, with seat-bound sex following very much in second place. In fact it tends to be the opposite. Aircraft lavatories really are very difficult places to have any sort of sex, apart from oral. Spatially they look like you should be able to do quite a lot if one partner kneels down, but the state of these lavatories after about the first thirty minutes in the air means that no sane person would get down on their knees unless they were wearing a wet suit. And wet suits are dead hard to screw in.

Also there is the enormous problem of getting both of you into the lavatory without attracting too much attention. Put three hundred people in the air for more than three hours and all they want to do is go to the lavatory. The result is incessant queues, all watching each other, vigilant for people trying to barge in or take longer than they're strictly allowed.

To make things worse, high altitudes bring out not just the urine in people, but also the snitch. If you walk into a lavatory with a partner and somebody else queuing sees, you can bet your complimentary airline magazine that they'll tell on you. This always ends in tears with a steward banging on the door, causing even more of a public spectacle, and then you and your partner having to exit in front of the whole plane.

So the key to lavatory sex seems to be, get in early, and restrict yourself to low visibility times.

Inside you can really do whatever you want, although simple practicality favours heavy petting to fourth base. The standard fantasy generally has the girl sitting up on the basin, although these are getting smaller, and the taps sharper, so a good deal of care needs to be taken. Others feature bending over the bowl area and standing on the bowl. It's really up to your imagination.

It's interesting to note that just as it's often quite hard to urinate when you're in air turbulence and the plane is rocking all over the place (something to do with an ingrown fear of spraying around the lavatory seat when other people are about to follow you in), it's also hard to handle your erection effectively in turbulence. The lack of balance tends to get him all moody, and can sometimes drive him away altogether.

Sex on the seat seems so much more exposed, and altogether less probable, which is probably why the movie-makers have relegated it to second place. Yet in fact it is much easier. Obviously you can't do it sitting in a row packed with people. However, in economy the seats are so close together that it's actually quite hard to see what's going on, particularly when the lights are off or the movie's on. Here you really are restricted to heavy petting, but it can get very heavy indeed. Blankets and pillows provide great camouflage and generally one partner does things to the other under the blanket while the recipient looks around, trying to appear as normal as possible. What keeps the activity so quiet is that anybody who does see what's going on actually can't believe it, particularly on largely British flights. The same instinct that would make someone too embarrassed to tell a stewardess there's a sealed bag, sitting alone, ticking in the back of the plane in case it's just an alarm clock, also applies to suspicions of covert oral sex in 31B.

Much kudos attaches to being a member of the Mile High Club, even though the only thing that proves membership is your word. An attempt was made a few years back to try and make membership contigent on having photographic evidence. But the logistical problems of having a photographer in the lavatory at the same time as the two lovers proved too great. In fact, however, there is a lesser branch of the club which, although on the surface less glamorous, actually takes risks, both physical and moral, which are every bit as great. They are the Mile High Masturbators – seriously!

This large and rambling organization is a collection of the most adventurous masturbators in the world. Men who have had one off the wrist in the most extraordinary of places, the peak of Anapurna, the bathrooms of French countesses, the corner of Hereford Square. If you feel yourself becoming depressed by your lack of success at having sex in extraordinary places, masturbating in them is an excellent second. It can be very gratifying, and very exciting, with all the piquancy of potential discovery as well as the gratification of exotic lust.

CHAPTER 12

Falling in Love

All through history mankind has tried to capture the feeling of falling and being in love. Scientists have tried to isolate it chemically, musicians have tried to express it symphonically, artists have tried to convey it visually.

But for the more humble concerns of this book we shall return to the skidmark, and the lavatory, and the bathroom cabinet to illustrate the feeling to potential victims.

When you're in love with someone, or falling in love with someone, skidmarks, wind, even your space in the cabinet simply don't exist. It's the same with bad breath and spots. They cease to be noticed. Physical imperfection melts away.

Falling out of love

Using the same humble yardstick, falling out of love begins to happen the very moment you notice that first skidmark, or smell that first discreet fart under the duvet, or catch that first blast of morning breath. Physical imperfection rushes back with all the inexorability of a bad cheque. And love's a gonner.

Living Together

The art of living together is a complicated one, and though in the west we regard ourselves as a very liberated society, we generally mess it up with about the same frequency as those we might consider rather more primitive.

Take the Maoris. There is an old Maori saying which comes from deep in the south island of New Zealand, which says, 'When you go to live with a woman, there are three main flashpoints. First, the lavatory. Second, your underpants. Third, the bathroom cabinet.'

Shearing away all the pop psychology, and woman's magazine truisms, these three fundamental Maori points prove remarkably effective.

The lavatory

Never, ever, go to the lavatory in the presence of your partner. There are no hairs to be split on this one. 'I'm only taking a pee' is not good enough. Don't do it. It's impossible to look attractive on the lavatory. It doesn't matter how much you love someone, how much you care for them, once you have seen them going to the lavatory, something, somewhere, just cracks and dies. You'll never be able to look at them in quite the same way again.

You know it's bad instinctively to be public about the lavatory, that's why such care is taken at dinner parties only to aim the urine at the porcelain sides of the bowl and run it as quietly as possible down to the water, rather than just splash in from a great height, or trying to ease the faeces gently down the bowl rather than risk the great crash as it breaks the water's surface from a full drop. Why don't we ever see scenes from 'Dynasty' with lavatories? Because they're uncool.

SCENE: MANSION, DAY

(*Alexis enters.*)

ALEXIS: Blake? Blake? Where are you?

BLAKE (V.O.): I'm in the lavatory, hang on, I'll be right with you.

(*Alexis picks her teeth as the sound of GRUNTINGS and SPLASHES comes from the lavatory.*)

(*Amanda and Krystle run in.*)

AMANDA: Daddy, Krystle and I have decided to be friends. Alexis, where's Blake?
ALEXIS: In the lavatory.
KRYSTLE: God, I'm dying too, HURRY UP, BLAKE.
(*The lavatory flushes. Blake walks in, zipping himself up. Krystle kisses him and goes to the lavatory.*)
KRYSTLE (V.O.): Oh god, Blake, you could have used the air freshener.
(*Sound of her spraying the stench with Dynasty Collection air freshener.*)
BLAKE: So Amanda, Alexis, you decided to come out here after all?
(*From the lavatory we hear the slightly higher-pitched grunts of Krystle.*)
ALEXIS: Don't fish, Blake, Amanda is here on her own accord.
AMANDA: It's true, Daddy....
(*The sound of heavy splashes from the lavatory then the spraying of air freshener.*)
AMANDA: Krystle and I have decided to be friends.
(*The lavatory flushes and Krystle enters, smoothing down her skirt.*)
KRYSTLE: That's better. Now, let's go and have something to drink.

Underpants

In much the same way dirty underpants should always be carefully slipped into the bottom of the laundry pile. This is the second axiom. If there's a major skidmark showing on a pair of pants don't ever leave them hanging visibly from the top of the laundry pile. This is one stage removed from the lavatory but it is tarred with the same brush.

Dirty underwear should be kept as private as possible. Your mum doesn't mind because she's seen so much of it. Your partner hasn't been blessed with those years of sympathetic nappy handling. She won't look on them favourably.

The Bathroom Cabinet

The jokes men used to make about women moving into their homes and inexorably taking over all their cupboard, drawer, and finally bathroom cabinet space used to be fairly relaxed. It was all simple, tension-free fun because men didn't really have that much stuff. They were amused by the mass of cosmetic, clinical and couture equipment which their womenfolk seemed to require. But they enjoyed the results and it didn't really matter because they couldn't use the space themselves.

Now everything has changed.

Men have almost as much equipment as women, clothes, shoes, and accessories in the bedroom cupboards, and moisturisers, showers, after-shave, hair gel, hair dryers, combs, dental floss, mouthwash and everything else in the bathroom cabinet.

Space is no longer a joke. It's a battlefield.

Sometimes the results are terrifying. Take this tale of a submariner and his air stewardess girlfriend.

'The one big drawback about submarines is that you get a lot of piles. It's the days of sitting down. So at home I always keep a tube of pile ointment in the bathroom for when they get really sore.'

His girlfriend takes up the story:

'The stuff's called Anusol, it's thick and brown, but it's also in a tube which doesn't look so different from the ointment I was using for a small patch of fungus which had infected my breast. I mean in the light of day on a normal clear-headed morning they didn't look the same, but through bloodshot eyes and a hangover at five in the morning, they were identical.

So I ended up applying the pile treatment to my breast for almost a month, and he was spreading thrush ointment on his piles. We could have killed each other!'

The story is a terrifying one. But the health risk is only

Sex tip no. 32: Going to the Lavatory

Whatever happens, however loud your bowels are calling for relief, never, ever, go to the lavatory to do anything more than urinate if you're at a girl's flat or house who you are trying to win. One of the most pernicious of the Sod's Laws of sex is that the one time you defecate in an important date's flat, the lavatory won't flush. This is so desperately embarrassing it doesn't even bear thinking about. You stand in the lavatory, staring at the unmoving faeces, bobbing happily about in the Harpic, sneering back at you. The chances are if it was a heavy session you will already have been in there for quite a while which means that the girl will be wondering how much you are exactly doing (and no matter how much she likes you, images of people sitting on the lavatory are not attractive). This means that the clock is running on you. All you can do is sit out the two minutes it takes for the lavatory to refill and then flush it again, hoping that this time they'll disappear. Even if they do, she'll have heard you flushing twice so you've still got some explaining to do. Just do it at the restaurant or before you go out. Spare yourself the anguish.

---

the beginning of bathroom cabinet problems. It's also an emotional flashpoint.

Look at the times of day you're in the bathroom, using the cabinet. First thing in the morning, when you're in a hurry and bad-tempered. And last thing at night, when you're tired and bad-tempered.

Then look at the purpose of the things you put in the cabinet. . . . Vain things to make you look prettier but which you like to keep private.

Medical things to deal with periods and rashes and spots (embarrassing by their very nature), and then washing things like toothbrushes and flannels, which you tend to get very proprietorial about.

Mix these raw nerves up and you get trouble.

SCENE: BATHROOM, EARLY MORNING

(John staggers in, rubbing the sleep from his eyes. He stares into the mirror.)

JOHN: Oh god, I look awful.

(Karen follows him into the bathroom.)

KAREN: John, can I use the basin first? I've got to wash my hair.

JOHN: Oh shit, Karen, I'm late – couldn't you have got up earlier?

KAREN: Oh, like you always do, right?

(John starts cleaning his teeth over the bath.)

JOHN; Oh my god. Oh fucking hell. That's disgusting. You filthy bitch!

KAREN: What?

JOHN: You've left tampons or something on the side of the batn.

KAREN: Actually, Dr Spock, they're cotton wool pads, for taking make-up off.

JOHN: Oh.

(He looks at Karen.)

JOHN: Well, I wish you'd lose some weight, and THAT'S MY FLANNEL DON'T PUT IT THERE!!

KAREN (*starting to cry*): THAT'S IT, I CAN'T TAKE THIS ANY MORE. I'M LEAVING.

And you wonder why people get heart attacks when all that happens before the day's even begun. One researcher at the University of California did a comparative study of the number of emotional explosions in a standard twenty-minute period on the major prime time TV soaps, and the number of emotional flare-ups in the same time in average couples' bathrooms. Real-life bathrooms beat the soaps by a mile. Axiom three, sort out the cabinet.

Sex and Parents

There really isn't any great mystery to the handling of sex and parents. Some sexual prima donnas speak in hushed tones of their inability to perform the night they took a girl home and took advantage of their parents' absence to use their double bed.

But what's the big deal?

The key is to handle your parents' knowledge of your sexual life in the same way you handle knowledge of theirs. You just try not to make it too obvious. Don't rub it in anyone's face. No one really likes to think of their parents humping away madly upstairs, doing oral sex (Oral sex? My mum?), dressing up (Rubberwear? My dad?) and all the rest of it. So you just don't think about it.

It's the same with parents and your sex life. They don't want to think about it, they don't want to find out about it. Basically you can do what you want as long as you're discreet. The only real sin is being found out. That's just awkward for everyone. As long as appearances are preserved, there's no problem. So, for instance, there should never be any question of a major family row about you not being allowed to sleep with your girlfriend under their roof. Make up her bed in the spare room willingly with your mother, and the moment your dad turns out the light, you sneak along to do what everyone knew you were going to do anyway. Just don't acknowledge it.

Parents with sons tend to be more flexible about this than parents with daughters.

If you get discovered by the parents of a girl you're having sex with, then you could admittedly be in for a lot of trouble. If it's her father who discovers you, you could be in for the Haringey Chainsaw Massacre. The key here is to behave exactly as you would if discovered being unfaithful by a wife or girlfriend. Deny everything.

It doesn't matter what you say, there's going to be lots of shouting, fierce threats, and a lot of tears whatever happens. The important thing is to avoid the physical violence.

It's not too hard though because your excuses don't have to make sense. They don't need a logic of their own. It's the quantity of excuses not the quality that counts in these situations. You see he doesn't want to believe what he's just seen. His mind is desperately clutching at any straws of believable hope to prove his eyes wrong. He's basically on your side. Your job is to do everything in your power to support any illusions he seems to cling to. Massaging her back, making the bed, dusting off the duvet, reading together, say anything, and keep saying them until he calms down. With the girl helping too, and most probably the mother as well, most fathers will be pacified long enough to get you out of the front door. Don't worry what time of night it is, any mugger and any weather is better than breakfast with a suspicious father the next morning.

SCENE: BREAKFAST ROOM, DAY

(The boy, the girl he's just laid, the mother, and the father are sitting at the table.)

FATHER: Sleep well, then, Kevin?

KEVIN: Very well, thanks, Mr Soames.

FATHER: Strange, you look tired.

KEVIN: Oh no, not at all. I slept like a log.

MOTHER: More toast, dear?

FATHER: You look tired too, Jane.

JANE: No, really Daddy, not at all.

FATHER: That wasn't you I heard up in the night then?

JANE: No, not me.

MOTHER: Tea, dear?

KEVIN: Well, if you'll excuse me I'll be off.

FATHER: That's all right, Kevin, I'm driving in to town. You can come with me.

KEVIN: Oh no, I couldn't possibly.

FATHER: No, Kevin, I insist. Then we can talk about this.

(He holds up a used Durex.)

FATHER: I found it in the bathroom lavatory this morning.
JANE: Oh Kevin, I told you they don't flush away, they never do.
MOTHER: Cereal anyone?

Sex tip no. 33: Durex Disposability

Used rubber johnnies will not flush away unaided. They just inflate and then keep bobbing back to the surface. You have to wrap them in several layers of lavatory paper and then scrunch them firmly up. Even then they can sometimes float back. Always check that they have been fully flushed if their discovery is liable to get you into trouble.

Getting Married

Just as men are having to learn how to do the female things as well as the women with regard to looks, so they must now, if the male sex is to survive as a sex with any integrity, do the same with marriage.

Myth has it that females are the weaker sex, the more emotional, the more romantic. This is of course rubbish. Females are far colder and more calculating. They are more complex emotionally, they have so many feelings, and each one is so sophisticated that they can't carry the volume of feeling whicn the meagre collection of male feelings carry. The result is they think more and get carried away less when the pressure is really on. Nowhere is this truer than when it comes to choosing a partner for marriage. Women have an uncanny ability to be in love with a man and at the same time coldly assess him in terms of the material comfort he can supply, his ability as a homemaker, his potential as a husband. Men, remarkably, even though they are supposed to be the ones who coldly choose the woman who's going to make the right wife, are incredibly naïve when it comes to all this. They fall in love with a girl and want to bring everything to her her, they want to provide, so they don't mind if the girl has nothing, in fact it's better if she has nothing because then they don't feel threatened in their role as provider.

This is stupid and outdated. We must move with the times, we must learn to look at partners in terms of their ability to provide too. Otherwise we're lost. Just look at Ali McGraw in *Love Story* to get an idea of how sophisticated the females have already become at this. She's dating Ryan O'Neil, he's rich as shit, but has started worrying (naïvely masculine) about whether she's in love with him or his money. They pull up in his convertible sports car outside a massive country house owned by his family, and he turns to Ali McGraw, a tear in his eye:

O'NEIL: Listen, I've got to know, is it me? (*He turns and gestures at the house.*) Or is it my family, my background, my money?

Ali McGraw's answer is a self-interested work of art.

McGRAW: I can't answer that. Don't you understand? You wouldn't be you without all of this. It is you.

The man and his money are inseparable. This is such a clever answer, and this really is the way women think when they are considering marriage. You must think like that too. What are her career prospects? Are you always going to be paying for her?

CHAPTER 13

Boredom

It's almost impossible to believe. In fact it is impossible to believe. But the fact of the matter is that no matter how beautiful, how willing, how perfect the girl is, sex does eventually become boring.

Jerry Hall says that she slips on stockings and suspenders to keep Mick Jagger entertained in bed, you know, to stop him getting bored.

BORED!!?!

BY JERRY HALL!??!

Yes, bored by Jerry Hall. Eventually it becomes routine. The edge goes off it. You miss one night, then another, then pretty soon you're going for a week, maybe two, without doing it.

Has your sex drive gone away?

No, you still look at girls on the Tube and try and imagine them doing oral sex. You still gaze at dirty magazines. You still masturbate.

But having sex with your partner?

It becomes a bit like cleaning your teeth.

So what's there to do?

Many things. But most of all, doing it in different places. Showers, aircraft, trains, baths, everywhere. What are the drawbacks? What are the advantages? A special team of Sex Tips investigators filed the following reports.

Showers

Another staple of the soft porn movie and magazine (do you remember Vanessa Williams?). Compared to the bath it's a dream, for both sex and masturbation but like all waterbound activity comes with very real problems. The first is the lack of friction.

It's only when it's not there that you realize how important friction actually is. If you take two, wet and soaped bodies then try and make them hold onto each other for some serious groping or sex, you're rapidly in the casualty department unless you're very careful. Everything slides about. This is quite pleasant when it's a case of a breast in a hand, rather like playing find the soap, but when it's a case of a foot on the tiles, or both arms round a waist for support, it gets really aggravating.

Tip No. 1: Leave out the soap and shampoo if you've actually decided on full sex in the shower.

The second thing about sex in the shower is that it has to be done standing up, and the problem with standing up is that unless you're perfectly matched heights, the man has to hold the woman around his waist. This is tough on a thick carpet. On a wet shower floor it's impossible.

The third thing about sex in the shower is that you get cold if you don't get enough of the shower. There's nothing worse than that lovely warm tingle of water all over your body, and then long bouts of standing unsplashed in a bathroom draught.

Don't even think about sex in the shower if your 'shower' is one of those hand-held things with a metal tube from the taps. One of you is always cold, and one of you always has to be holding their hand in the air.

The consensus of opinion is that you should have a good play in the shower beforehand and then go somewhere else to finish off. If you're just petting under the water, you don't have to worry about grip, soap, or friction. Even hand-held showers can be fun, because you don't have all the complicated mechanics at the end of it.

Getting into showers with clothes on is an enormous turn on but the drawback is that you have to do something with them when you're finished and it's so hard to get up for this sort of thing when you've just been hit by the post-orgasmic blues.

Washing each other can be great fun, as well as very hygienic but it can sometimes be a little revealing. If you've got an incipient bald patch which you've managed to keep pretty well hidden, it almost always comes out in the wash. Also there's a strict time limit. After about twenty minutes the wrinkles and blotches start to appear, in direct proportion to fading eroticism.

One of the greatest 'sex in the shower' clichés immortalized in the second *Shaft* movie, is the technique of gripping the rail of the shower curtain while bracing yourself for sex. The cliché is that the sensations are so pleasurable that though the rail drives into your hands, you notice nothing.

This has never happened. Ever. No shower curtain in the metallurgical history of the West has ever been able to withstand this sort of battering. Don't try it.

Baths

The only real drawbacks with baths is that they are always too small. If you've got one of those mammoth, semi-detached baths with room for a couple of rugby teams, then you are problem-free. You can thrash about with abandon, and do it horizontally, which makes everything so much easier. With more normal-size baths, one of you always has to have the end with the taps, or else try and squeeze in between the other's legs. After about the first two minutes you find yourself wishing that you were alone, and generally after about five you'll have a row and will be.

What seems to be a lot more effective is one person sitting in the bath and the other kneeling beside it, helping relax with their hands. After you've both had a turn in the water the sexual tingle and drowsiness is so great you're screaming out for the duvet and diaphragm.

Other parts of the house

The great thing about the living-room floor, or the kitchen wall units, or even the attic, is that though they tend to be intensely uncomfortable, they are very novel.

The key is not to plan for sex too much. Haul in mattresses, and towels, and pots of steaming water, and the novelty rather goes out of it. You've just shifted your bedroom into the kitchen. No, the whole thing has to be much more off the top of your head. You're in the middle of supper, or of cleaning the house, or of paying the bills, and you suddenly just fall on each other, letting the passion take the edge off the discomfort.

The only problem area is the kitchen floor, it's always got crumbs on it which makes you all itchy, and it also gives you the chance to look under the cooker which is always a depressing sight with its dried souvenirs of the last five years' meals. If you are worried about making a mess on the carpet or the furniture, take one piece of toilet paper from the bathroom. No more. It's like packing. The longer you wait in the bathroom thinking about it, the more you'll end up taking.

Other parts of the house (postscript)

It's worth noting that the rug in front of the fire is a vastly overrated spot. You just fry after about ten minutes. And whenever you try moving away you start getting cold. D. H. Lawrence was a great theorist but lacked a strong grasp of the practical application of his methods.

CHAPTER 14

Jealousy/Infidelity

Emmanuelle 4 – Goodbye Emmanuelle may not seem the most obvious place to go to draw significant lessons about life and relationships, but it nevertheless has something important to say to the frustrated, red-faced male, trying to be an enlightened modern lover, caring about his girlfriend's independence, and never getting jealous.

The film opens with Emmanuelle bringing a secretary back to her husband as a birthday present, so that he can screw her in the shower. Her husband then brings a male friend back for her whom she screws on the beach, and so the series seems set to continue in its time-honoured vein. But ten minutes later Mr Emmanuelle, a model of sexual enlightenment, is consumed by jealousy. After four Emmanuelles, twenty one rip-off spin-offs, and a series of eleven books in which he and his wife happily mess about with anyone who comes their way, this ultimate of open relationships falls to pieces. The most mythically enlightened man in pornographic history gets jealous.

This tells us something. That being jealous is as instinctive as masturbating.

So what do you do?

Not this. . . .

(*Traditional man trying to be enlightened about his woman.*)

MALE: Good morning, darling. Mmmmh, I slept really well last night.

FEMALE: Oh good.

MALE: But, gosh, you must really have worked late.
FEMALE: No.
MALE (*fishing*): Oh, well, I've got to admit I really did begin to worry when you didn't get back till late. Still, there you go. . . .
FEMALE: Yuh.
MALE (*pauses, then*): You know, I think it's really important in a relationship that you can always tell your partner everything. You know, not feel that if you go out one evening with a man that you wouldn't be able to tell me because I'd get all possessive. That's just awful.
FEMALE: Do you really think so?
MALE: Oh yeah, god, otherwise everything's just so stiff and awkward.
FEMALE: I went out with Jeremy from the office last night. He took me for a meal and then we went dancing.
MALE: YOU FUCKING BITCH I KNEW THERE WAS SOMETHING GOING ON. HOW COULD YOU DO THAT TO ME AFTER ALL I'VE DONE FOR YOU?

The frustrating thing for the male is that the less jealous and possessive you are, the more girls will like you. The more you don't care where they've been, who they've been there with, and how much they like them, the more they'll be willing to wrap themselves around your little finger. But it's a virtually impossible task not to care.

So what tends to happen is that the male gets angry, indignant, and gets ready to argue. He dresses up his jealousy in logic, it becomes a fair-minded complaint about his girlfriend's uncaring behaviour. He starts the argument and the girl is laughing. She sees right through the logic dressing, the open-mindedness, and knows that he's jealous. This immediately means a big swing of power to the girl's side.

Arguing with a girl when you're jealous is next to impossible.

They have a unique weapon which we shall refer to as schizophrenic memory. They have an uncanny ability to recall every last detail of when you phoned her, when she phoned you, what you said and what she said. The result is that you lose your side of the argument. She runs rings round your attempts to manipulate the circumstantial evidence to make her appear wrong. The male tactic is generally to persuade the girl that she is guilty, to induce her to throw herself at his feet and plead for forgiveness for doing anything to hurt such a good and kindly man.

Once you've lost you are then still wracked by the pangs of jealousy but they are made even more intense by losing the argument, and now you can't even sulk visibly because you know it won't win a victory. So you have to assume a good-natured, good loser attitude, while she just forgets it immediately. She remembers enough of the facts to win the argument, and then can forget it all (no matter how bitter) so that it doesn't hang like a dark cloud over the rest of her evening.

So how do you argue with a girl?

The answer is you don't argue. It doesn't matter how great the temptation gets, how bitter the feelings of jealousy, how suspicious the circumstantial evidence. DON'T show that you're jealous. The fact is that there are two types of jealousy; effective jealousy and ineffective jealousy. Ineffective jealousy shouts, sulks, and shows that it's under its girlfriend's thumb. Effective jealousy is Old Testament in its nature. It doesn't speak, it acts.

If she has gone out for a long, candlelit dinner, *á deux*, with a man who fancies her, and you can feel yourself getting all wound up DON'T show it. Be nice and friendly when she gets back and just carry on as normal. Ask the odd question, but basically act as if you're really not that interested. Then go out for a dinner *á deux*, with a girl that she thinks fancies you (this could be any girl she doesn't know). If you don't know any other girls just pretend to go out for a meal with a girl. If she goes to a party, for drinks, to play tennis, whatever, make sure you always duplicate it, that you do the same. This way the independent portions of your lives stay equal. She'll hate this, and once you've got into the swing of it, you'll start feeling less jealous. The result is, you win.

If you can, if she's gone out on a date which is making you feel particularly bad, go out yourself on the same evening and don't get back until after her, preferably after she's gone to bed. She'll come back expecting you to have waited up for her (if you're living together), or to have waited for her call (if you don't) and find that you're out enjoying yourself. This restores the balance too.

Is jealousy a bad thing?

Of course it isn't. Like a good row it keeps things ticking over briskly, and keeps you interested.

The only sort of jealousy that you should try and avoid like the plague is 'dog in the manger' jealousy.

If you've stopped going out with a girl, you mustn't get into the habit of hating other people having her. This drives you insane in a matter of weeks. Throw your energy into someone else as fast as possible.

Infidelity

Should you or shouldn't you?

Well, of course you shouldn't. If you're going out with someone it's bad. If you're engaged to someone, it's very bad. And if you're married to someone, it's bloody awful. But given that you've got to try not to be unfaithful, there will be times when the temptation just gets too much and you succumb. What should you do?

First of all, at all costs, don't get her pregnant. It doesn't matter how impolite you have to be, don't take any chances on contraceptives on a one-night stand. Use as many as you can fit on or in.

Second, never admit it.

There's a terrible fallacy that somehow as long as a couple can share everything, it will all be okay, and that if they can't there's something terribly wrong with a relationship. This is completely wrong. In fact it's bullshit.

Some things should never be shared and infidelity is one of them. The fact is that men, and a growing number of women, can have sex with someone else and not feel any less strongly about their partner. But they could never explain it without making it seem so bad it would ruin everything. So the answer is to say nothing, and deny everything. Even if your girlfriend catches you naked in bed, in the act, with another woman, deny it. No matter how improbable the excuse, looking for your keys, helping her with her bad back, anything, but deny it. Your girlfriend or wife will never really believe you, but the fact of your infidelity is shunted into a sort of limbo somewhere between proven and unproved. As long as you don't flinch through the tears and accusations, you'll be okay. Stay firm and lie like hell. The moment she hears you admit it, it's all over.

What about if you suspect your girlfriend or wife of infidelity? No problem. This comes right back to the jealousy section. All this business of looking for tights worn a different way round at the end of the day, regular handwritten letters on the breakfast table from some strange postal district where you have no relatives, or sudden attempts at smartening herself up, going to health clubs, doing her hair, it's all a waste of time. If you really start looking for all that it'll drive you into a frenzy of jealousy. It's a bit like chocolate or a dirty magazine, you just can't put it down. When you find yourself getting suspicious, never argue and start watching, make a point of doing just the opposite.

Care less, but start doing the same stuff yourself. Go to the health club, write yourself letters, go on mysterious dates, wear your tights on the wrong way round when you come in at night. Copy her and any trouble will be cured.

CHAPTER 15

Dear John Letters

The 'Dear John' letter has such a mammoth history it's hard to know where to begin. For thousands of years women have been dropping men by mail, almost since the first letter was ever delivered (there is some evidence to suggest that the first letter ever delivered was in fact a 'Dear John' letter). Dropping someone with a letter is like asking someone out with a note, a wimp's response to a difficult situation, but as with the note it can be an effective method. They can say exactly what they mean, they can say it carefully so as not to make it sting too much, and it does avoid all those tears and recriminations.

However, in recent years the full 'Dear John' has given way to an altogether more insidious version. This is the 'semi-Dear John', a note, letter or card, generally sent when the girl is away on holiday, which prepares you for the end, without actually delivering the bullet itself. Men must learn to identify these notes, they must learn to read between the lines, to interpret the slight nuances, the subtleties of meaning, and pick up the signal fast. Because for all their insidiousness, these 'semi-Dear Johns' do at least give you the opportunity to save some face and not be there when she comes back, thereby avoiding the necessity for a full dropping.

Let's look at two examples.

She's gone on holiday, somewhere hot. You're not sure how it's going. You're waiting for a card. She's been away two days in the first instance, then this card arrives:

Dear John
I really mean it when I say 'the weather is wonderful and I wish you were here'. I'm getting a good tan and seeing a lot of the island. Most evenings I spend in the local bistro whch is great and very traditional with not too many holidaymakers. I'm getting plenty of sleep so I shall be well rested when I return. I think this is just what I needed, to wind down and relax. I hope you are looking after yourself, not too many takeaways. I can't wait to see you, lots of love, *Sharon*

Okay. This is a thoroughly positive letter. The fact that it may be a pack of lies, that she's out with locals messing about every night, hasn't been to bed before 2 a.m. and then often not on her own, and all the rest of it doesn't matter. Her intent is clear, to make you feel good. It's arrived early which means that she's been thinking of you from the start, it's signed 'lots of love' which is significant (the signing off is always a vital sign), it makes an explicit reference to your domestic arrangements, implying that she'd like to be looking after you. A good postcard.

Now the bad card. It arrives on day 10 of her holiday.

Dear John
Everything is perfect, excellent weather, good food and wine, and lots to do. I thought holidays were for resting but I seem to have been out partying every night. The locals really do look after you, especially English girls! I know all the best night spots and we go every night, during the day the most I can manage is to lie in the sun and work on the tan. Luckily all the holidaymakers are young and I've made loads of new friends. It will be a terrible drag coming back to the monotony and weather of England. Oh well! See you soon.

Sharon

Right, this is really bad. First, it's not signed 'love Sharon'. It's impossible to leave love out of a postcard unless you're making a conscious decision not to put it in.

If it isn't there it's not there for a reason. It's telling you something.

The card didn't arrive until well into her second week. This means that she wasn't thinking of you at all. She's also made lots of new friends among the other holiday-makers, as well as getting on very well with the locals. She's telling you that she's messing about, or at least is behaving like a single girl on holiday. The jokes with exclamation marks after them always convey something special. In this case it means. 'I'm screwing them'. Finally, she's not looking forward to coming back. The correct response to this card is to assume it's all over. Don't call her when she gets back, and if she calls you, play it very cool. Let her make any running that's left.

Getting Dropped and Doing the Dropping

Here's how every man would like to think he'd drop his girlfriend:

FEMALE (*stretching*): Aaaahhh, oohh, good morning, darling.
MACHO MALE (*yawning*): It's all over. Fuck off.
FEMALE: Yes, but, you can't. . . .
MACHO MALE: There's a door in this room, use it.

Here's how most men actually drop their girlfriends.

FEMALE (*stretching*): Ahhh, ohhh, good morning, darling.
MALE: Er, hi, oh, look, darling, I think we need to talk.
FEMALE: Talk? Oh, you mean about dinner tonight, with my parents.
MALE: Well, yes, about that too, but also we need to chat about. . . .
FEMALE: Sorry darling, I'm in a terrible rush this morning, let's talk later.
MALE: No, honestly, I mean, this is serious, it's just that. . . .

FEMALE: Bye, see you later.
MALE: Yuh, okay.

Eighteen months of attempted chats then ensue until this conversation:

FEMALE: But I just don't think there is anything wrong with us.
MALE: Look, I just can't stand being around you, hurting you like I do. I care about you too much.
FEMALE: I don't hurt.
MALE: Oh, you say that, but I'm just not good enough, I'm so afraid we'll ruin everything, then I'll lose my best friend.
FEMALE: Then what are we talking about?
MALE (*panicking now*): It's not yoú, it's just circumstances, they're ganging up against us, I know that if I carry on I'll see you get hurt.
FEMALE: Does this mean you don't love me any more?
MALE: Of course I still love you. I just never want to see you again.

The reason there are fifty ways to leave your lover is because men through the ages have wimped out of actually coming straight to the point and saying it. Women are generally far better at it than men.

MALE: Hi, I've brought you these flowers, how are you?
FEMALE: It's no good pretending any more. It's all over. I'm sorry. Goodbye.
MALE: Oh, huh, yuh.

And there's no doubt about it that the faster it is, the more merciful it is. Getting the bullet always hurts like hell so it's better to make the firing squad as brief as possible, rather than drag it out with repeated flesh wounds.

Once you've dropped someone it's only fair to stay clear of her friends for a while, even if you're much closer to them since you started going out with her. In fact you're probably well advised to steer clear for a while because

Sex tip no. 34: Does It Hurt Most Being Dropped or Doing the Dropping?

'God, it's so hard having to drop someone. I just wish they'd always drop me.' Does it hurt more being the victim or the executioner? There's absolutely no question about this. 'The executioner hurt more' line is a sexual version of the 'this is going to hurt you more than it's going to hurt me' one. In other words it's 100 per cent pure bullshit. Nothing, no guilt, no resentment by your ex's friends, no subsequent regrets, are as bad as the sting of being dumped. It's ignominious and it's painful, and the fewer times it happens the better.

---

the sympathy is nearly always with the dropped, not the dropper, and only the most selfless of partners can resist a minor revenge campaign.

If you've been dropped it's just a matter of regaining your confidence and starting all over again. This happens naturally so it's really not worth worrying about it too much. The one thought which has provided the most solace to the embittered dropped male over the centuries is a simple one. Sit down somewhere quiet, summon up a mental picture of your ex, and then say to yourself, 'I'll age better than you'.

This works really rather well.

CHAPTER 16

Doing-It-Yourself

Masturbation is the ultimate male common denominator. It's a stirring thought that for centuries, all over the world, men with nothing in common, not a language, not a moral system, not women, not even a clothes sense or hit parade, have all taken the same pleasure from rubbing their penises. In caves, in igloos, and in bathrooms all over the world, men are masturbating AT THIS MOMENT.

Don't ever knock it. Masturbation makes Christianity or Marxism look parochial.

And what are the most frequently asked questions by the masturbating hordes themselves?

First, is it healthy?
Second, do women do it too?

They're important questions and need to be answered. Basically unless you're doing it very badly, masturbating is no problem. It actually builds up sexual stamina and is a pleasant way of killing a few idle moments which you'll never tire of. Just try and think how many other activities you could do two or three times a week for a whole lifetime (and for free!) and still not get bored with? Even the greatest literature and the greatest music pale in comparison to the hand shandy.

There is, of course, a downside, but this needs to be considered in strict sequence.

A Brief Survey of the Significance of Masturbation

Legend has it that masturbation, not the spare rib or the serpent's quick-thinking, was what led man to look slightly differently at woman. Somewhere, sometime, some adolescent cave boy was playing absent-mindedly with some rocks in his lap when he discovered that every time he rubbed one on his penis it felt good. He rubbed it more, and the more he rubbed it the better it felt. For days he amused himself this way, afraid to tell any of his cave friends in case the magic went away or they laughed.

Then, one day, he ejaculated.

He was shocked. Terribly shocked. He thought he must have burst some inner organ, and took to his bed for the rest of the week, waiting for the terrible illness to strike. But it didn't. And remembering the rather pleasant feeling he'd had when he ejaculated, he did it again.

Soon he was getting very expert, doing it twice, even three times a day, but gradually the initial excitement wore off. Until he happened one day to be down by the river and saw two cave girls taking off their mammoth skins and playing in the water. Suddenly the thought struck him, 'how nice it would be if one of those girls masturbated for me'. So he discovered sex, and the rest is history.

What makes the history unusual is that women never really learnt how to masturbate a man properly. For all the male's centuries of chauvinistic sexual greed, and clitoral incompetence, he has nevertheless by and large been far more proficient at dealing manually with a vagina than the female sex has with the penis. Somehow they just can't get it right. The angle's all wrong, they hold it in the wrong place, they pull down on the skin at the top too hard. The whole thing's a complete disaster which the male just has to grit his teeth through and smile because he knows how embarrassed the girl will be if he stops her right away. Let's face it, after 2000 years you'd think the female sex would have learnt, and it's not as if it's small and elusive like the clitoris. You can hardly miss an erect penis.

Do women do it?

Yes, they do, though not in quite the same massive, instinctive numbers. However, what makes a lot of female masturbation interesting is that their technique can be fundamentally different. Sometimes they have fantasies while they do it, but just as often they will just lie back and enjoy the feeling without trying to think dirty thoughts.

Men can never do this, or rarely. Only technical purists normally have the strength of mind. Which is a shame because the great advantage of doing it without thinking dirty thoughts is that you can focus your mind completely on the sensations involved.

It's not being cluttered by images of women throwing themselves at you. There's nothing wrong with fantasies (or fanasties as they call very unpleasant fantasies) but they do tend to dictate the pace of the wrist action. If you can just concentrate on how it feels you can often get a much better sensation because you're more awake to what's going on. But the moment you start doing it the temptation to start squeezing in a dirty thought or two is almost too strong to be ignored. Next time, you think, and the experiment's over.

Masturbating techniques

When a chap first starts his overriding concern is not to be discovered. He still can't really control what's going on down there and can't really judge how far the ejaculation is going to leap. So he'll normally be standing behind his bedroom cupboard door, trousers on, but unzipped, or sitting on his bed, trousers round his ankles.

There's nothing wrong with either of these methods, bedroom masturbation is fine, as long as you've got tissue paper with you. If you don't, and often one doesn't ('I won't actually go the whole way, I'll just play around a bit'), you must bear in mind that you've got to get to the bathroom undiscovered when you've finished. This is far more difficult than you at first imagine. When you come you'll catch it in the hand that's been doing the masturbating, sort of boxing everything into a closed fist cupped over the top of your penis. From that moment you've got about forty-five seconds of dribble-free time to get to a tissue. With only one hand free it's hard to get your trousers back up and held tightly while you make for the bathroom. So you leave them round your ankles and have to shuffle, one hand clutching at the dribbling penis, all the way to the lavatory roll.

If there are stairs between you and the paper, forget it.

If you get discovered now your loss of face is so great it doesn't bear thinking about.

Generally, if you're going for a bedroom wank get the tissue in first and lock the door, or better, go to the bathroom itself. It's actually far nicer not to have to hold back and start worrying about carpets, trousers and everything else, but just let it all burst forth into the Doulton bowl. One word of warning about bathrooms though is that if you take dirty mags in you must remember to take them out again. It's very easy, in the post-orgasmic glow, to tidy yourself up, zip everything back in, and then walk out leaving the map there. Sod's Law makes sure that it's the most embarrassing person who finds the mag later.

The bath and shower are equally popular sites. There's something about 2½ gallons of hot water that turns the male mind relentlessly to sex, but again both come with drawbacks. Say you're in the bath, and you've started to masturbate. The first problem is that the regular little splishing noises don't sound anything like washing. They sound like masturbating.

There's no two ways about this. So you've either got to take the radio in and turn it up, or else start running the tap in the sink.

Once you've ejaculated the real problems start. Sperm

is slippery when it's dry, and fairly hard to handle, but nothing compared to what happens when it's submerged in water. It immediately turns into long strands of viscous thread which float eerily around the bath and seem to zero in on the hairiest bits of your body. The moment they touch they hook on with every little bit of drowned sperm and won't let go. The more you try to flick it off, the more encased it becomes. As it gradually dries, it gets a used chewing gum texture and is impossible to get off.

Some men prefer to wait until they've got out of the bath and then masturbate into the water, but frankly you may as well do it over the lavatory. This way you get too cold anyway.

Others stand up while the water's still in the bath, then step out and drain it all away down the plughole. But again you get cold, and the sperm has a way of strapping onto your ankles faster than you can say spermicidal jelly.

Showers are generally a lot easier, because you haven't got to worry about the sperm floating around for too long. One school of masturbators firmly believes that masturbating while kneeling on the shower floor is the ultimate sexual experience. Drawbacks are that if the sperm does hit you, the pressure of the water spray turns it to glue very fast. And also, in the super-sensitive state of the post-orgasmic penis, high pressure streams of H_20 are agonizing.

In both instances you need to check that the sperm has filtered away down the plughole at the end. If you leave it on the porcelain or the tiles it turns a yellow, mucous colour and is so obviously sperm it's impossible to talk your way out of it.

There is one very advanced and rarely performed masturbatory technique which sexual historians believe was brought to the west with the return of the first Christian missionaries from China. A highly complicated and sometimes painful technique its advocates claim for it quite astonishing results.

The ancients called it, 'The Sleeping Beauty'.

You know those nights when you wake up suddenly and find one of your limbs riddled with pins and needles because you've slept on it awkwardly. Well, the first prerequisite of 'The Sleeping Beauty' is that your good arm should be so afflicted. This involves getting it in a difficult position, curled up under you as you prepare to go to sleep.

As soon as it's lost all normal feeling you then have to wrap your dead fingers around your penis in the masturbatory grip you prefer (you normally have to use your other hand to wrap them on) and then begin to go to it, gently, otherwise your hand falls off and you have to start again.

The astonishing thing is that it actually feels like someone else, with an insider's knowledge of rhythm and grip, is doing it to you.

Being discovered

Most regular masturbators have been discovered at least once in their lives, a horrific experience which is carried bitterly to the grave. There's something about self-abuse which feels dirty and wimpish. It doesn't matter how enlightened you are, or how macho you are, it's excruciating.

A bit like being caught with another woman, you must never admit what you're doing. One of the great advantages of doing it sitting down as opposed to standing up is that you can immediately bend over and reach with both hands down to your ankles. This effectively covers the offending zone and you can explain away the lowered trousers by pretending to investigate for a suspected verucca or a scratch between the toes.

Frequency

There's nothing terribly wrong with very frequent masturbation except it can rather tire you out and leave your penis feeling so desensitized even the boldest of grapplings only come through your nervous system as if through two thick wet suits. The more you do it, the less good it feels. Three times a week, with gaps in between, is about ideal.

Masturbating with Aids

This means dirty phone calls, dirty magazines, or dirty videos. All the numbers you can call to have a woman speak dirty to you are in America and this addictive habit rapidly makes cocaine look cheap. Forget it.

Magazines and videos certainly provide an added dimension. The problem is less how to use them, which is mostly instinctive, and more how to buy them.

Let's start with magazines.

With middle-of-the-road pornography, the type that's on sale in newsagents, the same feelings of embarrassment will occur as with contraceptive purchases. Some men get these feelings so acutely that they try and shoplift the dirty mag in question by wrapping it up in a newspaper and only paying for that. This is a dreadful ploy. How a man can risk being discovered shoplifting a dirty mag rather than the simple alternative of just gritting his teeth and buying it, is beyond belief. Most men have tried something like this though, at some point in their sexual careers. It is an adequate sign of the strength of the drive to masturbate, but not a good method. There is a better way.

First, choose the right newsagents, NOT the corner shop where you go for milk, the staple for all your locals and friends. And not the familiar vendor at the Tube or bus stop on your way to work. These are regular places where you need to be comfortable; you are a familiar face and can't afford to be caught out there. Choose a shop a little off the normal beaten track.

Don't hesitate once you're in the shop. Save all the hesitation for outside. Try and go in, stall, walk away a few times, pluck up some more courage, but once you're in go straight for the dirty magazines. The key here is not to waste time looking at the sports mags, darting glances at the top shelf, next to the amateur photography section. Once you've been browsing and stalling for ten minutes it's going to be so obvious when you eventually grab the mag and rush to the cash register that you're as embarrassed as ever. No, the right thing to do is this. Go in, pick up a newspaper (this takes the edge off the mag) and then select a mag. Don't flick through it, this is too tawdry for words. Then go to the cash register using the paper to hide your purchase in the event of there being a queue. Always have the exact money ready so you can hand it over and leave fast.

The same rule applies to video rental shops, only instead of buying a newspaper, make an inquiry about renewing your membership as you hand the video you want over, to take off the edge.

Sex shops are much easier all round. The only problem here is getting up enough courage to go in. Once inside everyone just gets on with it, there's no pretence because there's nothing but pure porn there.

Magazines are especially good for masturbating – you flick through them fast, find the bit you like, and then concentrate on it for the final burst. But videos can be unhealthy. Because they go on for quite a while the temptation is to masturbate again and again and again, and the result is that you become incredibly stale and sex-hungry at the same time. It's almost as if your appetite has lost the ability to be sated. This can happen with mags too if you have a huge pile of them. Masturbate more than twice in a row and you're rapidly propelled into this sexual limbo. You're left pacing around your house, tired, exhausted, but still throbbing with the scraps of passion, unable to make it all go away. If it's a video the whole thing is made worse by the fact that you've had to wait for days for everyone else to go away so that you can watch it. The expectation puts everything on super edge. So with the video, experts suggest holding off from actually coming until at least two-thirds of the way through, and restricting yourself to just two gos in any one sitting.

Magazines can also have a limiting effect on your fantasizing ability after they've been around for a month or two. In fact you'll probably find that they increase the number of times you masturbate while decreasing the pleasure gained. The problem is that you get into a rut, you can't be bothered to think up something new and dirty, so you just fall back on the old mags even though you know them inside out. Boredom rapidly breaks out all over.

The pornographer's catch?

The problem with all dirty mags and videos is that they're always fairly frustrating because no matter how much they show, you always want more. If it's *Playboy* you wish it was *Penthouse*, if it's *Penthouse* you wish it was *Fiesta*, if it's *Fiesta* you wish it was *Experience*, if it's *Experience* you wish it was *Colour Climax*, and if it's *Colour Climax* you wish it was the *Colour Climax* video. In the long run you're always going to lose.

Sending off for magazines and videos

Receiving pornography and the assorted, extraordinary sex accessories which are currently advertised in the back sections of the pornographic press by post does seem like a good idea on the surface. It's so painless. You don't have to endure the embarrassment of asking for them, going into shops, queueing with them in your hand, standing face to face with sales assistants. However, it has some drawbacks. Even though the manufacturers always promise to send you whatever you've ordered under plain cover, your name and address can get put on a mailing list. When you walk into a shop, even though you're seen, you don't have to hand over your name, address, phone number and details of your credit cards. Just think for a moment if *Private Eye* were to print a list of all the merchandise you had received over the past twelve months, or about which you'd received literature. Fill in those forms and you commit your purchase permanently to history. You never know what might happen.

If you still prefer that risk to walking into shops and buying face to face then there are some simple precautions which you can take. Always pay by postal order, not cheque or credit card. Postal orders are more anonymous. If possible have the package sent to your parents' address and then forwarded with your name slightly misspelt as a red herring. They'll never guess because it's in plain wrapping paper. Never give phone numbers or business addresses.

Enlightened Pornography

You'll meet some men who profess a completely enlightened attitude to pornography. This doesn't mean they don't approve of it, or need it, rather that they are entirely unembarrassed by purchasing it or being seen to read it. You know those people you see brazenly browsing through the top shelf at airport newsagents, even scrutinizing centrefolds on the Tube.

If you can manage this level of enlightenment, good on you, you are spared much terrible anguish. However, for those aspiring to this state and venturing into it by slightly ironic gestures around their flats or houses (e.g., piles of dirty mags by the upstairs lavatory – this could either be for masturbating or for making you laugh by pretending to be for masturbating) there is one cardinal rule which should never be broken.

If a dirty magazine is to be left anywhere accessible at your home it should never have pages sticking together. A dirty magazine can be passed off with a dash of bravado. Stuck together pages cannot.

Discussing pornography

Simply never try and justify pornography. It's virtually impossible to do it. If someone brings up the subject the only acceptable side for an intelligent person with any degree of sensitivity to be on is the anti-pornographers'. Oppose them at your peril unless you're one of those vaguely Gallic looking worldly-wise men with a five o'clock shadow, and can argue moral confusion and aesthetic decadence and make it look cool.

Also available in Arrow

SEX TIPS FOR GIRLS

All the things your mother REALLY never told you . . .

Cynthia Heimel

'A witty send-up of all those dreary sex manuals, it tells you what you really want to know' SHIRLEY CONRAN

These are the times that try a girl's soul. Things have gone all weird in the world. Nobody can get a decent job, a good cigar, or a sane boyfriend. Most of the rock-and-roll played on the radio is by dead people. 'But what can I do about it?' you ask. Read on . . .

It is time to shun the trivial (eg tax shelters, home computer systems and designer sunglasses) and embrace the frivolous (eg drinking champagne, telling jokes and making love). It is time to give sex the respect it deserves. There are those who have been trying to take sex out of the realm of the frivolous and put it into the realm of the trivial. Those who think that romance is dead and that sex is just another biological function.

But romance is not dead. Sex is important. Sex is profound. And sex is funny.